# VERTEBRATES

# VERTEBRATES
## by Nathan Aaseng

A Venture Book
**FRANKLIN WATTS**
New York • Chicago • London • Toronto • Sydney

Photographs copyright ©: Animals Animals: pp. 11 top (W. Gregory
Brown), 11 bottom (G. I. Bernard), 16, 45, 51, 53 (all Zig Leszczynski),
20 (M. Austerman), 25 (Johnny Johnson), 29 (R. F. Head), 31 (Robert
Redden), 36 top, 79, 85, 87 (all Leonard Lee Rue III), 39, 63 (both Stephen
Dalton), 66 (Breck P. Kent), 74 (Mickey Gibson), 76 (Stan Schroeder),
83 (Stouffer Enterprises), 89 (F. Roche), 95 (Irene Vandermolen); Visuals
Unlimited/Cleveland P. Hickman, Jr.: p. 36 bottom; Photo Researchers/
Bucky and Avis Reeves: p. 49.

Library of Congress Cataloging-in-Publication Data

Aaseng, Nathan.
Vertebrates / Nathan Aaseng.
p.   cm.—(A Venture book)
Includes bibliographical references and index.
Summary: Examines fish, reptiles, mammals, and other animals with
backbones, noting both their similarities and their differences.
ISBN 0-531-12551-3
1. Vertebrates—Juvenile literature.   [1. Vertebrates.]
I. Title.
QL605.3.A2   1993
596—dc20       93-13391 CIP AC

# CONTENTS

To Jay, Maury,
Mikhaila, and Evan

# INTRODUCTION

Vertebrates make up only about 4 percent of the named animal species on earth. Yet if you ask people to draw a picture of an animal, they will almost certainly draw a vertebrate. Most of us consider vertebrates to be the state-of-the-art, luxury showroom models of the animal world. From the fish that glide through the water to the birds that soar through the air to the mammals that prowl the land, vertebrates dominate our view of the animal kingdom far more than their numbers would suggest.

Our world is home to such a bewildering variety of animals that biologists have had trouble sorting out and classifying them even on the broadest scale. The major groupings are called phyla (the singular form of the word is *phylum*), and experts claim there are anywhere from twenty to thirty-eight phyla, depending on which characteristics they judge to be most significant. Vertebrates are such a small part of the animal world that they are not even allotted an entire phylum to themselves. They are placed in the phylum *Chordata* along with a few strange aquatic animals such as the *tunicates,* or sea squirts.

Tunicates seem more like sponges or jellyfish than like the animals we call vertebrates. The adult form does not have a well-defined head. Like sponges, these animals anchor themselves in one spot. They feed by creating a water current with tiny hairs called cilia, and then filtering out the small food particles that float in that water. The juvenile, or larval, form of the tunicate, however, has an elastic rod known as a *notochord* that runs down the length of its back. Along this notochord runs a hollow nerve cord. The presence of nervous and supportive structures like these separates the chordates (the members of the phylum Chordata) from all other animals. The vertebrates are those animals in which this notochord/nerve cord feature has taken the form of a vertebral column, or backbone.

The backbone has two main functions that have served vertebrates well in their quest for survival. First, it provides strong support. One reason vertebrates have been able to develop larger bodies than other animals is that their backbone provides a sturdy framework that keeps the soft vital body organs from collapsing together in a heap. This support includes anchorage for muscles that provide the movement and flexibility animals need to get food and escape being eaten by other animals.

*(Facing page, top) Although the tunicate, or sea squirt, looks like an invertebrate such as a sponge or a cnidarian, its larval form does have a backbone.*

*(Right) This lizard skeleton clearly depicts the backbone, the distinguishing feature of vertebrates.*

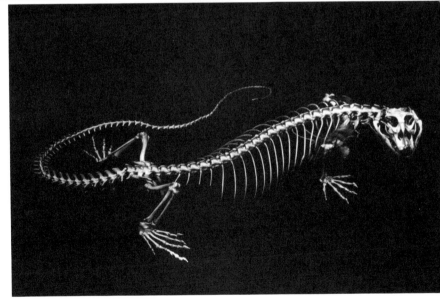

Many invertebrates, mollusks and insects being the main examples, also have a supportive structure, but this is an exoskeleton, a skeleton located on the outside of the body. The internal skeleton of the vertebrates provides the support and protection of an exoskeleton without the burden of its rigid, cumbersome outside shell.

Second, the vertebral column has been the framework around which a complex nervous system, consisting of a brain, a spinal cord, and well-developed nerves, has been developed. In addition to their size and flexibility, vertebrates enjoy a great advantage over other animals because of the ability of their nervous systems to collect, process, and act on information collected from their surroundings.

All vertebrates share a number of similarities other than backbones. Since they are mobile and move about in their environments, their sense detectors are more highly concentrated in the head—the part of the body that first encounters new environments. Vertebrates all have similar circulation systems so that their body cells can get the oxygen they need to convert food into energy. Each system has a heart made up of a special kind of muscle that is able to contract continuously without getting tired.

Vertebrates share a similar, multistage system of digestion. This consists of a mouth to take in food, one or more stomachs to digest it, intestines to further break down food into simple usable forms and absorb it into the bloodstream, and large intestines to reabsorb water used in the digestive process and to pass out waste.

Yet while vertebrates show many similarities, their members include such vastly different creatures as sunfish and ostriches. Vertebrates are among the most diverse of all animal phyla because of their success in adapting the basic vertebrate body plan to different needs. An animal living in the desert has very different survival requirements than an aquatic animal. An animal that feeds on plants has far different needs than an animal that eats rats. Creatures can survive better in a particular environment with a particular diet if they have developed features to cope specifically with their dietary needs. The tendency of animals to develop widely different features in response to environmental needs is called *adaptive radiation*.

Adaptive radiation has produced obvious differences in vertebrates, for example, scales in fish and reptiles, feathers in birds, hair in mammals. Based on some of these major differences, biologists have divided vertebrates into five major groups called classes: fish, amphibians, reptiles, birds, and mammals. The fish have recently been split into three groups so that there are now seven classes of vertebrates.

But within each class, adaptive radiation has shaped a wondrous variety of features, each of which gives a *species* a survival advantage. Mouths are shaped according to the most efficient means of eating particular foods. Legs and arms are shaped to provide speed, power, mobility, and dexterity. Physical appearance and various behaviors are tailored to increase an animal's chances of reproducing young.

There are three reasons to study the vertebrates as a group. The first is simply to satisfy our natural curiosity about the creatures, both familiar and unfamiliar, with whom we share the planet. Second, by studying the relationships among animals, we can gain a better understanding of our world. We can begin to see why animals are the way they are and why the world is the way it is.

Finally, studying the relationships among animals will help us to understand ourselves. By examining the ways in which our closest relatives in the animal world, the other vertebrates, have adapted to take advantage of survival opportunities, we can uncover clues as to where we fit into this marvelously complex world.

# 1
## FISH
— — —

With a few exceptions such as the sea horse and the rays, fish tend to look much like other fish. The basic fish form is a streamlined body equipped with fins rather than legs or feet. But this similarity in fish shapes should not lead us to believe that fish have not adapted much to their surroundings. They have in fact adapted so much and so well that there are about as many species of fish, nearly 30,000, as there are of all other vertebrates combined.

Fish tend to look alike because they are exclusively aquatic animals, and aquatic environments impose certain demands that a fish cannot escape. Water is 800 times denser than air. Because this density provides the advantage of support for an animal's weight, fish do not require muscles or limbs to hold them off the ground. But at the same time, the density of water presents a great deal of resistance to movement. The effect of water resistance is reduced with a *streamlined* body. Where a

*The popular sport fish, the largemouth bass,
shows the typical streamlined fish shape.*

fat, square-shaped fish would find it difficult to move against that resistance, a streamlined fish moves with relative ease. The ability to move is so important to a fish's survival that most fish have streamlined bodies.

Water also tends to be a more stable environment than the atmosphere. Temperatures, particularly in huge bodies of water such as the oceans, do not fluctuate wildly as they do on land. Land animals have to deal with periods of freezing or burning heat or extreme dryness or wetness. The absence of these weather conditions (except, of course, extreme wetness) and of abrupt environmental changes has limited the number of physical adaptations that fish have had to make.

If fish are confined to a streamlined appearance and have no need to adjust to drastic weather changes, then why have they branched out into such a large number of species? This contradiction can be partially explained by looking at where fish live. Roughly 97 percent of the water on earth is found in the oceans. Less than 1 percent of the water is contained in freshwater lakes and streams. If all the fish species in the world were divided equally among the waters of the world, 1 percent of the fish species would be found in fresh water. In reality, freshwater sources contain more than 40 percent of the world's fish species!

Why is this so? Because freshwater fish are isolated in small areas, whereas the ocean has few barriers to keep fish separate. In the ocean, successful adaptations made by an individual of any species tend to be shared among all fish of the species as they interbreed. Isolation, though, prevents a population of fish from sharing any favorable adaptations it might make with other members of its species. Eventually, two isolated populations of the same species may become so different that they become separate species.

Fish were the first vertebrates to appear on the earth. Fossils indicate that they have been in existence for 500 million years. The earliest fish were the *Agnatha*, the "jawless" fish. Only a few dozen species of Agnatha exist today, the most common of which are the lampreys. Lampreys spend most of their life as freshwater larvae called *ammocoetes*. Ammocoetes are similar to the early chordates from which the vertebrates arose. They are wormlike creatures with a notochord below their dorsal nerve. Ammocoetes live in burrows with their heads poking out and feed on tiny organisms that they filter out of the water by using their gills. A lamprey exists in this form for most of its life, up to seven years in some cases.

Eventually, the ammocoete transforms itself into an eel-like adult. This form has an internal skeleton made of cartilage. Unlike most fish, lampreys have no paired fins or scales. The stomach is absent—the esophagus leads directly to the intestines. Some adults do not even eat; they live only long enough to breed and die. Parasitic lampreys may live for a couple of years, often going out to sea and traveling many miles in search of prey. The mouth of a lamprey is adapted to its parasitic life-style. After sighting its prey, it attaches itself to the fish's side with suckers and rasps, or cuts, through the scales with sharp teeth arranged around its circular mouth. Lampreys remain attached, living on the blood of their prey.

Despite being one of the most primitive fish, lampreys are effective parasites. In recent decades, a series of canals built to aid shipping traffic between the Great Lakes and the Atlantic Ocean allowed sea lampreys to enter a new environment. The lampreys destroyed so many trout that they nearly ruined the entire Great Lakes fishing industry.

Apart from the lampreys, however, most of the jawless fish have died out. They have been replaced by fish with two important advantages: jaws that have been adapted in many ways to help in food collection and paired fins that have increased locomotion and maneuverability.

Of the fish living today, the first to display these characteristics were the *Chondrichthyes*. This group is made up of about 700 species of sharks, rays, and skates, which are distinguished from other jawed fishes by internal skeletons made of hard but flexible *cartilage* (instead of bone).

Sharks are well equipped for hunting. They locate food with a sense of smell so keen that they are able to detect the presence of a drop of blood diluted in 25 gallons (95 liters) of water. Smell detectors are concentrated in a pair of nostrils, and shark brains are largely devoted to processing aroma signals. Sharks also have pits on their heads that are so sensitive to electricity they can detect prey at short range just from the electric current produced by the prey's nervous system.

Once they have located food, the sharks' powerful muscles swiftly propel them through the water to reach their target. The mako shark is considered, along with the sailfish, the fastest swimmer in the sea, reaching speeds greater than 60 miles (100 km) per hour.

Sharks have powerful jaws equipped with sharp teeth for biting. They have many rows of teeth and can easily replace them. A single shark may use as many as 20,000 teeth in its lifetime. Twenty-five species of sharks have been known to attack humans, but only one species, the great white shark, regularly feeds on marine mammals.

Rays and skates are unusual among fish in that their bodies are flattened horizontally rather than vertically. This body shape is well suited for sweeping along the flat floor of the ocean, where many rays scavenge off dead animal matter that has sunk to the bottom. Some rays are predators that have developed extraordinary tools for catching food. Electric rays generate an electric current that can stun small fish. The sawfish's mouth resembles a chain saw and can be used to slash prey.

Reproduction is varied among the Chondrichthyes. Although sharks are among the oldest living vertebrates, the family has developed the technique of live birth. (The later-appearing mammals perfected that technique.) Rays are more traditional fishes in this respect. Most of them lay their eggs in cases attached to seaweed by long, coiled filaments.

The largest major grouping of fish, the *Osteichthyes*, includes the bony fish. Bone is usually a stronger supporting structure than cartilage because it consists of hard minerals in addition to living cells. Bone allows

*A shark's jaw can exert 300 times more pressure than a human jaw, and the fish's paired fins allow it to move quickly. These features make the shark a successful predator of the seas.*

these fish to have a better-developed spinal column—a true vertebral column with thin cartilage pads to provide cushioning between the vertebrae, the short sections of backbone. Along with this superior backbone comes a nervous system that is better developed than that of a shark. This includes well-developed eyes and a limited ability to learn from experience.

Whereas a shark hunts by smell, many of the bony

fish hunt by sight and are able to distinguish color patterns as well as shapes. The eyes can move up or down, and the lens can shift backward and forward to give the fish a wide field of vision.

Some fish such as carp and catfish feed on murky river and lake bottoms, where visibility may be poor. These fish tend to rely more on taste to locate food. They have *barbels*, long, thin projections that look like whiskers, located near the mouth. These allow them to feel and sample the bottom material to find edible food. Many fish also have taste receptors located on the outsides of their bodies, some even on the tail. While some other bony fish can hear little if anything, carp and catfish have excellent senses of hearing although they have no eardrum.

A unique feature of fish is a series of sensing devices called the *lateral line*. These sensing cells are sunk into a canal that runs the length of the fish's body about midway up its sides. Lateral lines can detect water turbulence caused by the motion of other organisms. Deep-sea fish that operate in the lightless depths and herring that feed on tiny floating organisms have especially sensitive lateral lines.

All these sensing abilities keep a fish alert to the world around it, and the developed nervous system allows it to respond to the information it receives.

Like the Chondrichthyes, bony fish breathe through special organs called gills. These delicate organs provide a large surface area for absorbing dissolved oxygen from water. They are thickly lined with blood vessels that transport the oxygen to the cells. Bony fish differ from sharks in that their gills are usually covered by a movable flap called the *operculum*.

Many Osteichthyes also have a device called an air bladder that helps them float in the water at a certain depth without having to use any muscles. Fish can fill the bladder with gas obtained from blood vessels to rise higher in the water, and can sink to a lower depth by expelling gas from the bladder.

Another difference between sharks and bony fish is the texture of the outside covering. The sharks' unusual scales give their skin a sandpaper texture that looks smooth from a distance. Most bony fish have thin, flat scales that are far more noticeable than shark scales.

Osteichthyes tend to be more streamlined than other fish. This is less noticeable in the sturgeon, one of the oldest of the bony fishes. Sturgeon grow to a considerable size, up to 1,800 pounds (800 kg) in some species, and have no enemies from which they need to escape. Their diet consists primarily of slow-moving mollusks, insect larvae, and crayfish, none of which require speed to catch. As a result, sturgeon have had no need to make particular adaptations for speed and remain rather heavy and cylindrically shaped.

Most other fish, however, require more mobility either for escaping predators or for obtaining food. Bony fish move by contracting muscles on alternate sides of their bodies so that the entire body bends in a sort of moving wave. Most of the muscles of a bony fish are devoted to this motion. The fins are not used for propelling the fish but for turning and stopping.

Predators among the Osteichthyes often have body shapes that provide them with hunting advantages. The long, narrow body shape of the freshwater pike, for example, is well suited for hiding. It allows the pike to nestle in among thick weeds as it lies in wait for fish, frogs, and even small birds and mammals to venture close. Its body presents a small target from the side, and so is difficult to spot. A moray eel needs a long, narrow body to maneuver among the coral reef crevices where it hides while waiting for octopuses and other prey to come within range.

A long body combined with a powerful tail also gives the freshwater pike and the ocean-faring barracuda an explosive burst of speed so they can strike before their prey has a chance to escape. Other fish, particularly plankton eaters, may be less powerful and more maneuverable so they can dart quickly from one side to another to nab food.

The Osteichthyes have jaws more flexible than those of sharks, and their mouths have been adapted in a number of ways to take advantage of special eating habits. Fish such as herring that eat small, floating plankton have no need of teeth. They simply gulp and swallow their small packets of nutrition.

Predators are often equipped with sharp teeth and larger mouths. Some deep-sea fish have teeth that point backward to prevent the prey from escaping. The anglerfish have especially long, needlelike teeth that fold back so they can close their jaws. The notorious piranhas have razor-sharp teeth and short, strong jaws for shearing off small pieces of flesh.

The mouths of bottom feeders are often located on the underside rather than pointing out toward the front. This makes it easier for them to root around and collect food in the bottom sediment.

The digestive system of a fish is tailored to meet its needs. Plants are more difficult materials to digest than animals. Those fish that include plants in their diet, particularly bottom feeders, have longer digestive tracts for processing their food.

Of course, animals must do more than provide for their personal survival; they must also ensure the continued survival of their species through reproduction. Virtually all vertebrate individuals are either male or female and reproduce sexually. In most fish species, the differences between males and females are not noticeable. A glaring exception to this is a variety of deep-sea anglerfish. The females of this species are perhaps twenty times longer than the males. The tiny male is unable to eat until he attaches himself to the female by his jaws.

At that time the two bodies fuse. The male loses most of his body systems and becomes little more than a parasite, but he is still able to produce sperm when the female needs it to fertilize her eggs.

Most bony fish, however, follow a more conventional pattern: A female lays eggs in the water and a male fertilizes those eggs shortly after they have been deposited. Methods of getting males and females together at the right time to complete this process vary with the species. For herring, which mass together in huge groups called *shoals* just before the females are ready to lay eggs, finding a male to fertilize eggs is no problem. More-solitary fish, such as pike, are drawn together by chemical attraction.

Among the fish, salmon have one of the more fascinating reproductive cycles. Adults make their way from the freshwater streams in which they were hatched to the ocean. There they spend several years feeding on other fish and growing rapidly. When they are ready to spawn, they combine an amazing memory with a keen sense of smell to locate the stream in which they were spawned. They then swim upstream, sometimes battling strong currents and jumping small rapids, to reach the spawning ground. The female matches up with a male and with her tail digs a long trench, often 10 feet (3 m) long and a foot (0.3 m) deep, in the gravel streambed. The pair lie beside each other in the spawning site, the female laying the eggs and the male following with sperm.

Because of the exhausting journey and the fact that salmon who have lived in the sea do not feed in fresh water, many salmon die shortly after spawning. The young salmon feed on the yolk of the egg and on insect larvae and the plankton that fed and multiplied on the dead parents. After a period of several years, depending on the species, they migrate to sea.

Migration to home spawning grounds is not unique

*Salmon swim against the strong current and
even jump up small waterfalls in an exhausting
effort to return to their spawning grounds.*

to salmon. Many European eels travel up to 4,000 miles (6,400 km) to reach their breeding grounds in the deep, warm waters of the Sargasso Sea.

There is no particular pattern as to where in the water fish eggs are likely to be found. Cod eggs float to the surface, where they are scattered by currents. Herring lay their eggs in masses on the sea floor. Pike prefer to deposit eggs among weed beds. One member of the catfish family leaps up to lay its eggs on overhanging rocks or leaves.

Wherever the eggs are placed, they are usually left to hatch on their own. These unprotected, defenseless bundles of nutrition make easy meals for a large number of predators, as do the young hatchlings. As a result, the chance of an egg's surviving to adulthood is low. Most fish make up for this by sheer force of numbers. Many species lay hundreds of thousands of eggs at a time; the female cod can produce several million eggs during a breeding period.

Producing eggs with little chance of survival is a waste of energy, and some bony fish show behaviors that reduce that waste. Sticklebacks, for example, lay only 50 to 100 eggs at a time. The male guards the female as she lays eggs in a bed of seaweed; he then continues to watch over the eggs. The male will even pick up a hatchling in its mouth and return it to the nest if it wanders too far. Some fish, such as guppies, keep the eggs inside their bodies and bear live young. The female sea horse, in an unusual twist of nature, puts the burden of birth on the father. She lays her eggs in a pouch in the male's abdomen, where the eggs develop until they hatch. The young of a number of fish swim into the mother's mouth when danger approaches. The bitterling resorts to a sort of foster care involving an entirely different kind of animal. The female lays its eggs in a bivalve mollusk, and the male fertilizes them there.

Like all vertebrate groups, fish have shown a remarkable ability to develop features that provide survival advantages. For example, the carp has overcome the problem of limited food supply by expanding its diet. Aided by a longer digestive tract, the carp will eat just about anything it can swallow, from algae and other plant matter to dead animals and decaying matter to mollusks and insects.

The development of specific color patterns is a more subtle physical feature that helps keep fish alive. Most fish have darker colors on the upper side and lighter colors on the lower side. This helps them to remain hidden both from animals above who are looking down into the darkness of the water, and animals below who are looking up toward the light. *Camouflage* is used in other ways. Such species as the toadfish are covered with warts and feathery growths that blend in well with their rocky surroundings beneath the water.

One of the most curious adaptive features of fish is the ability to produce their own light. More than a thousand species of fish have this property, called *bioluminescence*. The manner in which it is used depends on the environmental conditions. For a fish living in waters where light can barely penetrate, a dull glow can actually be a camouflage to disguise the shadow of the fish's body. This shadow would ordinarily show up against the light when viewed from underneath. Fish living in shallower waters may use light to find or attract food. Some anglerfish that inhabit very deep waters have a glowing lure that dangles from the top of their head. This brings curious fish in close, where the angler can catch them.

Fish have adapted to just about every conceivable condition in the aquatic world. Perch have adjusted so well to the cold temperatures of fresh water in the northern hemisphere that warm winters actually retard the development of their eggs. Bottom dwellers such as anglerfish have carved out a niche in the ocean depths.

Some of these bottom dwellers have gaping jaws and long, needlelike teeth. These make them effective predators of squid in their domains 2 miles (3 km) beneath the ocean's surface.

Deep-sea fish are not the only fish who have come to use darkness to their advantage. Catfish, with their sensitive barbels, like to feed at night, when they have a sensory advantage over other creatures. Three dozen species of fish have even penetrated remote pools of underground water. Living in lightless caves, many of these fish have lost the use of their eyes.

A small number of fish illustrate the adaptability of the animal group that paved the way for vertebrates to colonize the land. One of the major differences between aquatic and land environments is that the gills, which are so important in obtaining dissolved oxygen from water, do not work in air. Many fish have developed breathing methods to supplement their gills. When the oxygen content of the water is too low, they gain extra oxygen by gulping air that enters the bloodstream through a concentration of blood vessels in the throat region. A few fish, called lungfish, most of whom are now extinct, developed lungs to more efficiently pull in oxygen from air. Some lungfish have become so proficient at breathing air that they will die if deprived of it.

The ability to absorb oxygen from air as well as water gives a fish a survival advantage. During dry seasons, small bodies of water can begin to evaporate, leaving a low oxygen content in the water. A fish that can breathe air may be able to survive until the rains come.

Sometimes evaporation is so great that fish are stranded out of water altogether. Some African catfish, for example, move onto the flood plains to take advantage of the available food and lack of competition from other fish. When the flood plains dry up, they are often trapped in muddy wallows. In such cases, air-breathing lungs would be an even greater advantage. Some lung-

*Catfish get their name from the three pairs of barbels that look like cats' whiskers. They use these barbels to detect food on muddy river and lake bottoms.*

fish can survive long periods of drought by burrowing into mud and hibernating for up to three years until water returns.

Another major hindrance to fish moving onto the land is their lack of mobility. The muscular bodies and tails that propel the fish so easily through water are virtually useless out of water, where the thin air provides

29

nothing for them to push against. Ancient lungfish and lobe-fin fish, however, had fins that were much fleshier than the fins of most fish, and so were better suited to support the weight of the fish out of water. Those lobes may have helped the fish to crawl and, combined with air-breathing ability, could have allowed the fish to move from a dried-up body of water to a better, wetter environment.

Movement on land is achieved today by certain species of catfish that can crawl, lungfish that move by wiggling, and by certain perch that can actually climb trees. A fish called the mudskipper also has eyes adapted to land living. Mudskipper eyes sit on stems high above the head and give the fish sharp enough vision to catch flying insects out of the water. Adaptations such as these undoubtedly enabled aquatic vertebrates to move onto the land.

The bony fishes have branched out in so many directions that experts have a difficult time grouping and classifying them. To the casual observer, a sunfish may seem far more similar to a trout than to a sea horse. Yet both sunfish and sea horses are included under the general heading of *Acanthopterygii*, while trout are not. The Acanthopterygii include those fish whose fins are sup-

*The sea horse swims in a vertical position and can wrap its tail around seaweed to hold itself upright. Despite these features and its unusual appearance, it is classified with more typical fish such as sunfish because it shares the feature of fins supported by bony rays.*

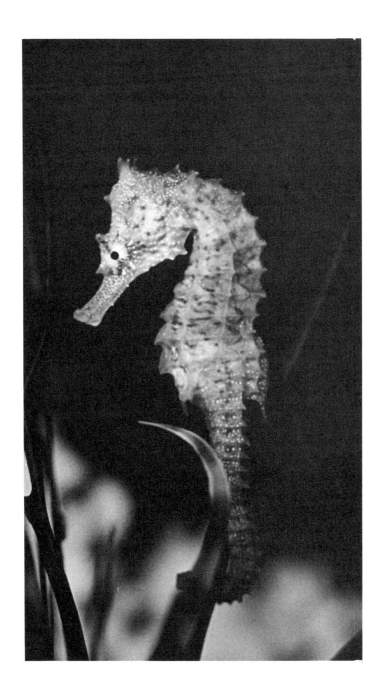

ported by bony rays, about half the total number of fish species.

The spiny-finned fishes are further divided into about a dozen orders. The most numerous of these are the Perciformes, or perchlike fish, which include about 8,000 species as varied as the freshwater walleye and the marine barracuda and sailfish. The largest order of fish without spiny scales are the Cypriniformes, of which carp are members, and Siluriformes, which include another bottom feeder, the catfish. Both orders contain more than 2,000 species.

Other fish orders that are important to humans for recreation and food are the Salminoformes (about 300 species of salmon, pike, and trout), Anguilliformes (about 600 species of eels), Clupeiformes (about 300 species, including herring), and Gadiformes (about 500 species, including cod).

As the dominant animal of the aquatic environment, fish as a group are in no danger of extinction. The majority of them live in oceans, an environment so vast that it is difficult to imagine that it could suffer from the impact of humans in any way at all. The most popular freshwater fish are avidly protected and nurtured by fishing enthusiasts.

Recent experience has shown, however, that the ocean and its fish have limits to the amount of abuse they can tolerate from humans. During the past century, even the great shoals of herring and sardine have been overfished, reducing fish populations drastically. Pollution and habitat destruction threaten the existence of many species of freshwater fish. In the future humans will have to practice wise conservation habits to ensure that the rich variety of fish life continues.

# 2
## AMPHIBIANS

Amphibians are the smallest group of vertebrates. Except for their use as dissecting specimens in biology laboratories and in an occasional frog-leg dinner, they have little economic value to humans.

Yet amphibians are fascinating creatures because they pioneered the way for vertebrates to move into an entirely new frontier. Four hundred million years ago, the only vertebrates were the aquatic fish. Sometime during the next several million years, some of the lobe-finned fishes left the water to live at least part of their lives on land.

Why would a fish, whose body is far better suited to living in water, choose to live on land? Some scientists believe that this did not happen by choice. They think that, during a long period of uncertain weather, many lakes and streams dried up. Under these circumstances, those fish who were able to wriggle out of the mud and stay alive long enough to get to a new body of water had a better chance of surviving. Gradually, according to this scenario, these fishes became more and more adapted to living on land.

Other biologists believe that the first land vertebrates moved out of the water by choice to exploit a new environment. Insects, worms, snails, and other invertebrates were already living on land. A fish with the ability to tolerate brief periods out of the water would find a ready source of food on dry land. This food was there for the taking, with few competitors to get in the way. Better yet, this was a safe environment, since all of the fish's natural predators were left behind in the water. These advantages were so great that even a vertebrate awkwardly suited for land life might find favorable conditions for survival there.

In either case, these first land vertebrates gradually evolved more favorable characteristics for land life. This happened because those individuals with longer legs, better lungs, and so on, survived better than others. The most favorable traits for terrestrial life were then passed on to the next generation. Over the course of time, animals developed in vastly different ways depending on what traits proved to be most favorable in a particular environment.

Amphibians are the oldest descendants of those first terrestrial vertebrates. In the days when they had no vertebrate competitors on land, there were many more species of amphibians than are alive today. Only three orders are still in existence. The most common amphibians are the *Anura*, the "tailless ones." This group consists of frogs and toads, and includes close to 3,000 species. This group is common throughout the world, but the vast majority is found in the warm tropical regions of Africa and South America. Frogs are generally distinguished from toads by their long legs and smooth skin. Toads tend to be heavier and rounder, with shorter legs and warty skin. Both have forelegs that are smaller than their rear legs. Anurans feed primarily on insects, which they snap up with their long, sticky tongues.

Less numerous are the *Urodela*, about 350 species of salamanders and newts. These creatures have four legs of equal size. They are common in the wetlands and woodlands of northern Europe and eastern North America and can also be found in parts of Asia and South America. All are carnivorous, feeding on animals such as slugs, worms, insects, and crustaceans, which they grab in their jaws. Although they have teeth, these serve to prevent prey from escaping and are not used in chewing.

The third group, the *Apoda*, or "legless ones," includes 150 known species of aquatic or burrowing amphibians found near the equator. Many of the underground species have no eyes, ears, or legs, and resemble earthworms. These slow-moving predators, which are also known as *caecilians*, eat mainly worms, termites, and insect larvae.

In many ways, amphibians closely resemble the fish from which they arose. For instance, the heart, brain, and digestive systems of amphibians and fish are similar. But a land environment poses a number of problems that fish never had to confront in an aquatic environment. In order to live successfully on land, amphibians had to find ways to cope with a host of new challenges that involved the need for support, mobility, respiration, retention of water, warmth, reproduction, and sensory ability.

Water, being far more dense than air, provides a great deal of support for aquatic animals. An animal moving from water to land needs better supportive structures to keep its soft body parts from collapsing, especially if it is to grow to any size. Amphibians gained the support they needed from their bone structure. The backbone serves as a sort of crossbeam on which the body is hung. This backbone, in turn, must be held up

Secretive salamanders (above) are seldom seen. Yet
some forested areas of the eastern United States
may contain a greater mass of salamanders than
birds and mammals. Newts (below) spend more
of their time in water than do salamanders.

by limbs. The lobe fins of the lungfish were not well suited to holding up the backbone. These were replaced by large limb bones that stuck out to the side and were held in place by muscles to provide a stable, four-cornered base.

The ability to move about is not essential to creatures in aquatic environments, where currents can often bring food to a stationary animal. Yet fish gained a survival advantage over other aquatic animals because of the quickness and agility that allowed them to actively capture food. Mobility is even more important on land, where food does not float about on currents.

Unfortunately for the newly emerging land vertebrates, the fins, the wave movement of the trunk and tail, and the streamlined, limbless shape that worked so well in water did not get them very far on land. The first land vertebrates found they could move best by pulling themselves along on their paired lobe fins. These short, weak appendages were designed for aquatic life and could produce only a slow crawl. Amphibians developed a better limb. As did the insects, which already thrived on land, they achieved the best results with jointed limbs that could provide more leverage and flexibility. More strength and leverage was added by attaching these limbs to the backbone. Early amphibians also developed digits at the ends of their limbs. These proved so useful that they have been retained by other vertebrate groups in the form of fingers and toes.

Salamanders and newts move one foot at a time when they walk: the right front, then the left rear, followed by the left front and then the right rear. At the same time, they have not abandoned the original swimming motion of the fish. When they walk, they curve their bodies in the same wavelike manner as fish, and they continue to swim in the old fish style. Salamanders are not able to run very fast, though, because of the way their legs project from the sides of their bodies. Much of their muscle is required just to hold up the body, and so less is available for moving the limbs. To get a feel for why salamanders cannot run fast, see how fast you can crawl with your arms spread out wide as opposed to crawling with your arms under your shoulders.

The Anura eventually developed a different method of transportation. Their back legs lengthened into powerful jumping limbs. Many frogs have become especially adept at leaping great distances by pushing off the ground with their hind legs and catching themselves with their shorter forearms as they land. With their longer legs and lighter bodies, frogs generally jump farther than toads. The tail, which serves as a stabilizing instrument in salamanders, would only be in the way in a squat-and-jump animal, and the Anurans are some of the few vertebrates to completely lose the tail.

Frogs, which spend a great deal of time in the water, have developed a different method of swimming than fish or salamanders. Rather than pushing against the water with their trunks, frogs kick out with their rear limbs. The adaptation of webbed feet to give their kick an even more powerful stroke provides them with excellent water mobility without hurting their jumping ability on land.

Some Anurans, particularly the spadefoot toad, have feet specialized for a different purpose—for digging quickly into the ground.

Perhaps the most obvious problem an aquatic animal has to contend with on land is respiration. Aquatic gills are designed to absorb oxygen from water, not from air. Like the lungfish, amphibians have developed a simple set of lungs to breathe in air. Frogs bring air into their lungs by opening and closing their nostrils while raising and lowering the roof of their mouth.

But amphibian lungs are too inefficient to provide the animal with its oxygen needs, and often play a minor role in respiration. Some salamanders, in fact, do not even have lungs. Amphibians rely on their skin to absorb

*The long extension of its rear legs provides the leopard frog with a tremendous leaping ability.*

oxygen directly from the air. This would be difficult if they were covered with the kind of nonporous protective scales seen on most fish. Instead, they have soft, moist skin that allows oxygen exchange, and many have mucous glands to keep the skin moist. Tiny blood vessels called capillaries lie just under the skin to collect the oxygen that is absorbed, and to pass along waste carbon dioxide to the outside. Salamanders that live primarily in the water often have wrinkled skin that provides more surface area for oxygen exchange. Amphibians can also absorb oxygen through blood-rich linings in the mouth and throat.

Amphibians have a circulation system similar to the fish's, except that their hearts have three chambers for pumping blood as opposed to two in fish. Fish hearts have no way to keep blood that contains oxygen from mixing with oxygen-depleted blood. As a result, they are continually recirculating through the body some blood that has not yet been supplied with oxygen. Amphibians are slightly more efficient because of partial barriers in the heart that help prevent blood that already contains oxygen from mixing with blood headed to the lungs for more oxygen.

Amphibians' various methods of respiring help them to survive in water, on land, and even underground for long periods of time. The inefficiency of these various systems, though, means that they are not able to sustain long periods of high activity. Amphibians spend most of their time resting and are active only in brief spurts. An inefficient respiratory system is also a factor in limiting the size of amphibians. Most are smaller than a human hand, the main exceptions being an African frog that weighs about 6 pounds (2.7 kg) and a giant salamander that can grow to nearly 5 feet (1.5 m).

Amphibian skin is a case of an animal giving up something in order to get something. Soft, moist skin may be ideal for oxygen exchange, but it also permits evaporation. Water loss is a major concern for animals moving to terrestrial environments, and the thin porous skin of most amphibians is a major liability.

Most amphibians have avoided water loss simply by staying close to water. Salamanders and newts, for example, do not live in deserts. Most Anurans live in the tropics, where humidity prevents drying out. Those amphibians that do stray from water avoid the sun, especially in warm weather, and spend most of their time in damp places under rocks and vegetation. The name "salamander" means "fire lizard" and comes from the fact that these animals were often seen crawling out of wood fires. While it appeared that they were produced by the flames, they were simply living in the logs that had been thrown onto the fire.

Toads that live in drier regions often burrow into the ground for most of the year and are active only during the rainy months. Despite their vulnerability to drying out, some toads can even survive in the desert. Some of them have evolved thicker skin at the expense of respiration. Some store water in a bladder and are able to withstand up to a 60 percent loss of body water. They do not drink water but have an incredible ability to absorb water through their skin. Some toads can take in water just from sitting on a damp patch of ground.

Extreme temperatures pose a far greater problem for terrestrial creatures than for aquatic animals. Like fish, amphibians are *cold-blooded* animals, which means that their body temperature is determined by the environment rather than an internal mechanism. This works well in aquatic environments, where the temperatures do not fluctuate a great deal. Moving onto land, where temperatures in one spot can range from well below 0 to over 100 degrees Fahrenheit ($-18°$ to $+38°C$), can be dangerous for a cold-blooded animal. Animals cannot function once their body temperature falls below or rises above a certain point. Amphibians have a further problem: In order to prevent water loss, most cannot warm themselves in the sun.

Amphibians have responded to cold weather by a kind of deep sleep known as *hibernation*. In colder climates, they spend the winter under logs or stones or in mud at the bottom of pools. With their body metabolism slowed down by the cold, hibernating frogs require no food other than that stored in their bodies, and can gain all the oxygen they need through their skin. Amphibians avoid overheating by staying in cool, dark, moist places.

Females protect their eggs from temperature extremes by producing ripe eggs only during the most favorable seasons. Amphibian eggs in warm ponds often separate, while eggs laid in cold water are often attached in a large clump to an object under the water. Bunched together, they retain more of the heat that their dark coloring absorbs from the sun.

The amphibians have adjusted to the challenges of temperature well enough that a few species can be found in even the harsher climates. Toads can be found in hot, dry deserts, two species of frogs live above the Arctic Circle, and another has been found 15,000 feet high in the mountains.

One of the most serious obstacles facing an animal moving from aquatic to terrestrial life is the matter of reproduction. Fish reproduce by laying eggs in the water; these eggs are then fertilized by males. The eggs are protected by soft, jellylike coverings and mature quickly. That system will not work on land without some major modifications. Air will not carry sperm to the eggs, the soft eggs are likely to dry out, and the fast maturing time restricts the ability of the embryo to develop all of the complex features terrestrial living requires.

Amphibians as a group did not evolve the elaborate changes needed to reproduce on land; most have simply returned to the water to accomplish this function. The name "amphibian" means "double life," and refers to the amphibian characteristic of spending the formative period as aquatic animals and the adult period as terrestrial animals. The difficulty of adapting aquatic breeding to a terrestrial life may explain why amphibians have developed the most diverse reproductive methods of all vertebrates.

Like all vertebrates, amphibians reproduce sexually.

The first task is to get males and females together to mate. Like fish returning to their spawning grounds, many male frogs find their way to their breeding ponds at the start of the mating season. They then emit loud croaking noises to attract females. This croaking also helps the females locate the right males, since a breeding pond may be shared by thousands of frogs from more than a dozen species. Some females also call males.

Once they have gathered in the same place, mating takes place. Salamanders often engage in courtship activities to stimulate the female into producing eggs. Some male frogs develop spiny swellings on their hands just before the mating season; these help them grasp female frogs to begin mating. Some male Anurans are so primed for mating during the breeding season that they will often jump on anything that moves.

Mating usually occurs in water, although some toads mate on land. Some fertilization resembles that of fish—females discharge eggs and males release sperm over them. In other cases, amphibians resemble later vertebrates—fertilization takes place in the female body. This occurs most commonly in salamanders. But since amphibians do not have a male structure for implanting sperm in the female, as later vertebrates do, the male deposits sperm on the ground or the bottom of pools; it is picked up there by the female.

As with fish, eggs are protected by a jellylike covering. Like fish eggs, amphibian eggs are highly prized as food by many predators and only a small number of them will survive to develop. Amphibians compensate by laying a great many eggs (although not as many as fish). Toads can lay 30,000 in a season.

Female frogs usually leave a pond immediately after laying eggs and retreat to a spot where they are less likely to be preyed upon. But other amphibians display parenting behavior that boosts their eggs' chances of survival. Some attach their eggs to leaves; some lay them on land, hidden in damp soil or under rocks. One kind of salamander will even lay eggs on the ceilings of caves. Some amphibians build nests, and in a few species the eggs stay in the mother's body and are born live. The female midwife toad lays her eggs on land and wraps them around the leg of the male for protection. Amphibian males in general are more commonly involved in caring for the eggs and young than are males of more recent vertebrate groups.

Tropical frogs often lay eggs in puddles or other small, temporary pools of water. This keeps them away from the usual aquatic egg eaters. Some species of African frogs lay their eggs on dry land near a river or stream. When the rains fall, the eggs hatch and the youngsters crawl into the water. A type of tree frog climbs down to the water to fill her bladder, then returns to the tree to lay her eggs. As the eggs are laid, she douses them with water from her bladder, and this swells their jellylike covering.

Perhaps the most fascinating aspect of amphibians is what happens to them in the weeks after hatching. The two-week period of development within the egg does not allow enough time to acquire the basic characteristics of an amphibian adult. The young develop through an aquatic larval stage first, during which they act more like fish than terrestrial creatures. Larval amphibians possess gills and swim about with the use of a tail. Anuran young, called tadpoles, have no legs.

Young salamanders and newts live on insects and insect larvae. Young Anurans are mainly plant eaters. Their small teeth are best suited for tearing away at algae and other aquatic plants, as well as occasional dead animal matter. Some species are filter feeders and can go through eight times their body weight in water per minute as they strain out tiny bits of plant matter.

After a period ranging from a few weeks to two years, the larvae go through *metamorphosis*, a startling change

The small, tufted gills of these wood frog
tadpoles will shrink and finally disappear
by the time the animals become adults.

in physical appearance similar to the way in which a
caterpillar changes into a butterfly. The physical changes
in young salamanders are subtler. The most noticeable
change is that their aquatic breathing organs—the gills—
are usually replaced by lungs, more terrestrial adaptations.

Frogs and toads, however, undergo drastic changes.
The gills change into lungs and the tail disappears. The

mouth widens and develops jaws. Legs begin to grow. The digestive tract, which must be long in tadpoles to process the plants they eat, shortens to as little as 15 percent of its original length. This happens in response to the more easily digested animal diet (mainly insects and worms) of adult frogs and toads. In one species of tropical frog, the tadpole is four times the size of the adult that eventually emerges from metamorphosis. All this change is triggered and regulated by a complex system of hormone glands. Frogs and toads continue to develop as adults until, at the age of three or four, they are capable of reproducing.

Like all vertebrates, amphibians have a specialized nervous system that gives them a survival advantage over many nonvertebrate animals. The larval forms have retained a lateral line, a feature of fish, for detecting motion in the water. Adult amphibians have chemical receptors scattered over their skin as well as smelling organs in the nose. These are more sensitive in salamanders and newts than in frogs. Amphibians also have a group of cells under the skin at the tops of their heads that are sensitive to light. Light receptors keep amphibians out of the sun, where their skins could dry up. They may also be important to the amphibians' sense of direction, and may help the animals find their breeding ponds.

Except for the caecilians, amphibians have large eyes that give them a good field of vision. Frogs and toads rely primarily on sight for detecting prey. Their eyes do not see shapes very well but are keen at detecting movement.

Salamanders and newts do not produce sounds and do not hear well, although they can feel ground vibrations. But frogs and toads were the first animals to develop a middle-ear cavity and a voice box. The production of sound and the ability to hear it is important in attracting and identifying members of their own species.

Except for some of the frogs whose long legs are

adapted for quick jumping, amphibians generally cannot move as quickly as most other land vertebrates. Neither do they have the size or teeth or sharp claws that would discourage a predator. Many amphibians, particularly toads, make up for these survival disadvantages by producing toxins. Some of these poisons simply make the amphibians taste so bad that no predator would want to eat them. Others are deadly. The poison-arrow frog contains one of the most lethal poisons found in nature. Poisonous amphibians are generally brightly colored so that predators will recognize them as poisonous and avoid them. The spiny newt has developed a unique defense against attack. It has sharp ribs that poke through pores in its skin whenever it is grabbed.

Amphibians are a dwindling group of animals. Some of this is because they have been outcompeted by other vertebrates better equipped to exploit the land environment amphibians once had to themselves. But the thriving Anurans have shown that there is a place in nature for animals with an amphibian life-style.

The greatest immediate dangers to amphibians are the result of human activity. Pollutants that poison the environment wreak havoc on amphibians. And because the prime amphibian habitats of swampland and tropical rain forests are some of the least favorable habitats for humans, these have been cleared away to make them more useful to humans. In doing this, economic developers have placed the survival of many amphibians at risk.

# 3
# REPTILES

Although the amphibians were the first vertebrates to venture onto dry land, the vast majority kept a lifeline to the water. That dependence on water presented an obstacle in taking full advantage of the range of possibilities of terrestrial life.

Somewhere around 300 million years ago, a group of amphibians made a complete break with their old aquatic life. These land pioneers became the first reptiles. Freed from the amphibian reliance on water, the reptiles dominated the continents of earth for a longer period of time than any other land vertebrate before or since. The reign of the giant reptile dinosaurs began about 280 million years ago and lasted for more than 200 million years.

Nature does not stand still, however, and the era of reptiles came to a close. The dinosaurs died out about 65 million years ago, and many other reptile species have become extinct. But there remains a diverse group of about 6,000 species of reptiles today, including

*Reptiles and amphibians that are now
extinct are re-created in this diorama.*

several holdovers from the dinosaur era. These animals
continue as the vertebrate masters of many desert environments where food is scarce.

One reason reptiles are especially fascinating is because they are believed to be the ancestors of both mam-

mals and birds. Their success in finding ways to adapt to a completely terrestrial life-style laid the groundwork for new groups of vertebrates that have flourished since the end of the dinosaurs.

Four distinct groups of reptiles—turtles, lizards, snakes, and crocodiles—are commonly recognized by their unique features. For experts trying to piece together the relationships between animals, however, the picture is not quite so simple. While they assign turtles and crocodiles to their separate orders, scientists combine lizards and snakes into a single order. A fourth order of reptiles, *Rhynchocephalia*, is made up of only one living species, the lizardlike tuatara.

The turtles and tortoises of the order Chelonia are easily distinguished by a unique protective shell made from the fusion of many bones. About 225 species remain of this order that has been around since the early days of the dinosaurs. Although some sea turtles spend almost all their time in the water, all turtles begin life on the land. Turtles are among the longest-lived animals on earth, with individuals of some species surviving well beyond 100 years. They range in size from a few ounces to the 1,500-pound (700 kg) bulk of the loggerhead sea turtle.

The vast majority of reptiles belong to the order *Squamata*. This includes about 3,000 species of lizards and 2,700 species of snakes. Most lizards are agile, land-dwelling creatures with long, slender bodies and four legs. Most are small, although the Komodo dragon can reach 10 feet (3 m) in length and 300 pounds (140 kg) in weight. Snakes have even longer, thinner bodies—some pythons have been measured at 30 feet (10 m). They lack the lizards' legs, external ear openings, and movable eyelids. Most live on land, but a few have returned to the water.

The *Crocodilia* order has some impressive family ties. The crocodiles, alligators, and gavials that make up this

*The Komodo dragon, the world's largest lizard,
was unknown to most of the world until 1912.
It lives on only a few small islands in Indonesia.*

order belong to the same group as the dinosaurs and are the last living link to those creatures. If, as some scientists believe, birds actually arose from that same group of reptiles, then crocodilians are the closest living relative of the birds. Only about two dozen species remain of this ancient order. Far from being primitive creatures that have somehow outlived their time, though, crocodilians are equipped with some advanced features that give them a survival advantage over many more recent arrivals. Modern crocodilians are not as large as some extinct species but can still grow to nearly 30 feet (9 m) in length.

Like the crocodile, the tuatara is a survivor of an ancient group of reptiles. It has a number of features—including extremely low body temperature, eggs that take fifteen months to hatch, and an eyespot on the top of the head—that distinguish it from other reptiles.

In order for reptiles to break away from the amphibian reliance on water, they had to change the birth and maturing processes. The quick-hatching, soft, jellylike eggs of the amphibians were not designed with dry land in mind. The covering offered too little protection from evaporation.

The feature that gave reptiles a clean break from the water was the shelled egg. It was not enough simply to have a waterproof shell to block evaporation. While putting up a barrier to water transfer, the egg somehow had to allow gas exchange in order for the animal inside to breathe. The shells of the reptiles contain vents that allow air to pass through the wall. Once the reptiles developed this type of egg, there was no going back. An amphibian egg is designed to absorb dissolved oxygen in water so as to sustain the life of the embryo inside it. But a reptile embryo growing in a waterproof egg laid in water would drown. The water would cut it off from the air, and the shell would prevent it from absorbing dissolved oxygen in water. As a result, today even aquatic reptiles such as sea turtles must return to the land to lay their eggs.

A few reptile species, however, broke away from their dependence on land for reproduction by keeping the developing egg inside the body and giving birth to live young. This is particularly true of the sea snakes, about three-fourths of which never leave the saltwater oceans. These creatures have, by bearing live young,

*This Northern Diamondback terrapin,
a member of the turtle family, is just
breaking out of its leathery shell.*

eliminated the need to come onto land in order to lay eggs. Live birth also occurs among reptiles in colder climates, where an egg would not provide the warmth the embryo needed for survival, and among boa constrictors, to protect the young from dehydration and fungus infection.

A disadvantage of reptile eggs is that the hard or leathery shell that offers protection from the outside also poses a barrier to the young animal when it is time to hatch. The young reptile has to be able to break through the shell to keep a comfortable nursery from turning into a tomb. Young reptiles are equipped with an "egg tooth" at the front of their mouths to penetrate the tough outer shell.

Reptiles eliminated the free-living larval stage of development by having their young develop for a longer period of time as embryos in the eggs. A long period of incubation leads to the problem of providing nourishment for the embryo during this crucial time of growth. Encased inside an egg, a developing reptile embryo cannot go out and collect food as an amphibian larva or tadpole can. But reptiles provide a food source inside the egg in the form of an enlarged yolk.

Moving the reproductive process onto dry land required a change in the mating behavior from that practiced in water. With no water to act as a transfer agent of sperm to eggs, fertilization must take place inside the animal. A few lizards produce young from unfertilized eggs, but this tends to be a long-term disadvantage to a species. Offspring of unfertilized eggs are identical to the parents. They do not display the variety of features that comes from a mixing of parental traits. Less variety means the species has fewer chances of adapting to environmental changes.

The vast majority of reptiles have developed sex organs that are able to accomplish internal fertilization. Reptiles have developed various behaviors that draw males and females together for this act. Sea turtles migrate, or home, to breeding grounds in a fashion similar to salmon and eels. They have an internal system of navigation that allows them to find their own small beach even after a trip of thousands of miles.

Terrestrial reptiles do not display the same type of homing. Many of them match up with members of the opposite sex on a more individual basis. Pairing between males and females is often aided by *sexual dimorphism*, which means that males and females are different in appearance. Males tend to be larger among land tortoises, crocodilians, and many lizards, while female sea turtles and snakes are generally larger than males. Reptiles that gain most of their information on their surroundings from their sense of sight, primarily the lizards, often show differences in color between the sexes, as well as minor differences in shape. Some male lizards take on especially brilliant colors during mating season to draw the attention of females. Snakes, however, have poor vision and must rely on their sense of smell to alert them to the presence of the opposite sex.

In some reptile species, most notably mud turtles and snapping turtles, the larger males mate by simply overpowering the females. But in most cases, internal fertilization requires cooperation between individuals of opposite sexes. Reptiles often encourage cooperation through courtship rituals such as head bobbing, tail thumping, or color displays.

Some male reptiles stake out their own territory, which they will defend against other males in breeding season. Larger and stronger males often hold more territory, and so are more likely to mate, a behavior that aids survival by passing on the genetic traits of the strongest members.

Timing of internal fertilization is not crucial for many reptiles. Some females are able to store the sperm for later use. A kind of turtle known as a terrapin can lay eggs four years after mating, and one species of snake has been known to lay eggs five years after mating.

Reptiles lay their eggs in a variety of inconspicuous places—sand, soil, vegetative debris, and rotting logs. Most adults play no part in the care and protection of their young after they lay the eggs. Sea turtles and some snakes may bury their eggs in sand to hide them from predators but offer no other protection. Crocodilians are an exception. The females of several species build nests in which they hide their eggs. The American alligator constructs a large mound of mud and piles of vegetation up to 10 feet (3 m) in diameter and 3 feet (0.9 m) in height. The rotting plants provide heat for incubation. The female guards the nest and even waters it during dry weather. When she hears noises from inside the eggs, she opens the nest so the young can crawl out. Pythons also protect their eggs by wrapping their coils around them and, after hatching occurs, may watch over the young for a while.

The protective shell and a longer incubation period give individual reptiles a greater chance of survival than amphibian eggs and hatchlings. As a result, reptiles do not use as much energy in producing eggs. Sea turtle hatchlings are at the greatest risk since they must plod across the sand back to the sea on limbs poorly suited to land locomotion. All during this trip they are exposed to predators, particularly birds. To boost the odds of some of these young surviving to adulthood, sea turtles may lay up to 200 eggs at a time. But even this pales against the millions of eggs laid by fish or the thousands by toads. Most reptiles lay only a dozen or so eggs. Iguanas commonly produce only one egg at a time.

Eggs were not the only amphibian carry-over from an aquatic life-style that fit poorly with life on land. Many amphibians' skins need to be wet in order for gas exchange to take place. These amphibians must be careful to keep their skins from drying out, and from allowing too much evaporation. Along with a waterproof egg, reptiles have developed a waterproof skin. Reptiles are covered with an outer layer of hard scales or leathery skin that prevents water evaporation. This allows them to venture out from the shadows and damp habitats to which most amphibians are confined.

Waterproof scales also allow reptiles to make use of a key source of energy not available to amphibians. Like amphibians, reptiles are cold-blooded animals that must rely on outside conditions to provide their body heat. Because their skins are generally not good at limiting water loss, amphibians must avoid the sun and so cannot absorb heat from that abundant source of energy. They have no way of quickly warming up. Since body systems operate more slowly when cold, amphibians tend to be sluggish much of the time.

Reptiles, however, do not have to worry as much about evaporation and so can bask in the sun to quickly raise their body temperatures. By alternately seeking sun and shade throughout the day, they are able to maintain an even body temperature.

Their use of the sun to generate warmth gives reptiles a great advantage in certain situations over *warm-blooded* animals (birds and mammals), which produce their own body heat. Much of the food eaten by a warm-blooded animal goes to maintain its body temperature. Reptiles, on the other hand, have no need to use food to generate body warmth. Biologists estimate that a reptile needs to eat only about 2 to 3 percent of the food required by a warm-blooded animal of similar size.

This is particularly important in places where food is scarce. Reptiles are often the dominant vertebrate species in desert locations where not enough food is available to support large bird or mammal populations. Reptiles survive the intense heat of the summer desert by being active only when the sun is down.

The disadvantage of being cold-blooded is that reptiles freed themselves from amphibian dependence on water only to be just as dependent on the warmth of the sun. Most reptiles live in warm climates. Only a few species of lizards, by making efficient use of sunning, can live in cold climates or in high mountains. Although a few species exist as far north as the Arctic Circle in Europe, reptiles do not exist in Alaska, Greenland, most of Canada, and parts of Russia.

In developing hard, waterproof skin, most reptiles,

with the exception of some aquatic turtles, have given up the ability to absorb oxygen through the skin. This trade-off could be made only if reptiles had a more efficient way of breathing, one that did not require gas diffusion. Reptiles gained respiration efficiency by improving on the poorly developed lungs of the amphibians. Their lungs are generally larger than amphibian lungs and have a greater surface area for absorbing oxygen from the air. Most reptiles pull air into their lungs by moving their ribs backward to enlarge the body cavity. Because of their restrictive shells, turtles cannot enlarge their body cavities. They must suck in air through contractions of special muscles in the upper legs and abdomen that create a sort of pumping action.

Crocodilians have developed the most efficient system among reptiles for getting oxygen to the cells. They have a thin membrane between the chest and abdomen that acts much like a mammalian diaphragm to bring in a greater amount of air. Crocodilians are the only reptiles to also have improved upon the three-chambered amphibian and reptile heart by adding a fourth chamber. The four-chambered heart separates blood on its way to the lungs from blood that has already been to the lungs to obtain oxygen. In this way, only oxygenated blood is pumped out to the rest of the body.

Reptile skeletons also show some adaptations to land life. Some reptiles protect their delicate vital organs with a set of bones, called ribs, on the underside. Many lizards have long necks that enable them to lift their heads well off the ground when crawling around on all fours. This improves their field of vision.

The most obvious skeletal variation among reptiles is found in the turtles. At some time during their evolution, turtles found a survival advantage in a protective suit of armor that completely encased the body. The benefits compensated for the loss of mobility caused by the heavy shell. The armor became even more of an advantage when turtles made room in the shell to withdraw softer parts, particularly the head.

A number of unusual structural changes were needed to accommodate this shell. The backbone, ribs, and many other bones had to be fused together to form the shell, and the turtles' shoulder blades and hips had to move into an alignment different from that of any other vertebrates. Their trunks also became shorter than those of other reptiles to keep the shell as small as possible while affording the greatest body coverage.

The protection provided by this unique body form has enabled turtles to survive for hundreds of millions of years, but it did not come without a cost. The severe limits imposed by the inflexible shell made it difficult for turtle bodies to adapt features in response to their environment. Turtles have not given rise to any other forms of animal, and the species that live today are much the same as turtles from 200 million years ago.

Aside from the turtles, however, reptiles have developed features that favor greater mobility. Lizard limbs are stronger and more flexible than those of amphibians and enable the creatures to scamper over the ground quickly. Crocodilian legs are placed closer to the body, which gives them better leverage. This means that less of their muscle is needed for supporting the body and that more can be used for motion. Not only can crocodilians run quickly over short distances on land, but they can also swim well with the aid of a large, muscular tail.

Snakes have lost their limbs, which at first glance seems to be a step backward in mobility. But snakes are believed to have come from a group of burrowing lizards who found the long, legless body form well designed for slithering through dense underbrush and other tight places. Most snakes move by contracting their muscles and pushing off against surfaces gripped by their scales. Larger, heavier snakes tend to move straight ahead, while smaller ones use a winding, whiplike motion. Far from being hindered by their lack of legs, many snakes can move about easily on land, swim, and even climb trees. The rat snake is so flexible and coordinated that it can wrap around and subdue three small mammals at once. Aquatic snakes, like all aquatic animals, overcome water resistance with a more streamlined body. Their heads are usually smaller and their tails thicker than those of land snakes.

One of the most obvious ways in which we see adaptive radiation is in the ways animals obtain food. Reptiles show a broad range of features that allow them to feed from a great variety of food sources.

Chameleons followed the same path as the frogs, snapping up insects with their long tongues. Most reptiles, though, developed an advantage over insect-eating amphibians by acquiring greater mobility and more powerful jaws. Most species of lizards continue to favor insects for their meals, seizing them with their jaws and teeth.

Over the course of time, reptiles adapted to other available forms of food. Marine iguanas eat algae that grow on ocean rocks. Some slow-moving turtles turned to more easily obtained foods such as plants, fruit, worms, and mollusks. Others used camouflage to draw victims within reach. The matamata of South America has a shell that looks like a collection of rocks and a wide head that blends in with aquatic bottoms. It sucks in unsuspecting fish that come to feed near it. The alligator snapping turtle holds its mouth wide open underwater to display a pink, wormlike projection that attracts fish. And the snapper blends into the background so well that fish swim into its mouth.

With their strong jaws and sharp teeth, the giant monitor lizards known as Komodo dragons can run down and kill mammals as large as goats. Crocodilians have even more powerful jaws and can eat fish, mammals, and even crack turtle shells. Their eyes and nostrils are well engineered to make them effective hunters. Both are located high on the face so they can remain out of the water even when the rest of the animal is submerged. This allows the animal to breathe and to sight prey while remaining hidden. And with their air passages unconnected to the mouth, crocodilians can open their mouths underwater to attack or eat prey without gulping water.

Snakes are predators that have evolved special adaptations for killing and eating animals. Some snakes wrap themselves around their prey and tighten their coils, causing the prey to suffocate. Other snakes kill by injecting prey with venom. The vipers, for example, have long, hollow fangs to inject their poison. These fangs fold up inside the mouth so that they do not pierce the snake's own mouth. Venom and constricting power allow snakes to subdue larger, more active, and more dangerous animals (including lizards, other snakes, birds, and small mammals) than they could otherwise safely overpower. Snakes that lack venom or the power to constrict prey have diets that are limited to smaller animals.

Because of their small heads and lack of chewing teeth, snakes would not be able to eat the larger prey they kill without some modifications of the jaw. Their jaws are loosely hinged so that they can open far wider than the snake's head. Snake respiratory systems are also designed so that sea snakes can swallow prey underwater and land snakes can breathe through a trachea in the front of their mouth even while their food passage is completely blocked by food.

Reptiles have developed various sense organs to collect information from their environments. Lizards generally have good eyesight for spotting prey. Crocodilians see well and are also well adapted for night vision. Snakes have a number of small sensory organs that compensate for the poor vision of their unblinking eyes. Pit vipers are so named for two small pits between the eye and nostril used to detect warmth. This helps the snakes locate warm-blooded mammals to attack and to find victims that have run off to die after having been poisoned.

Snakes also have a bundle of nerve endings known as a Jacobson's organ inside the roof of the mouth. This accounts for their keen sense of smell. Their flickering tongues sample the air for tiny particles, which they transfer to the Jacobson's organ, which then collects information from the sample.

Hearing varies among reptiles and is probably best in the lizards, which have ear openings. Crocodilians and a type of lizard called the gecko are among the few reptiles that emit loud sounds. Snakes and turtles do not produce calls, nor do they hear well. Snake charmers supposedly can put cobras in a trance by playing music, but cobras are actually deaf.

Reptiles display some unique survival features that have helped them compete for space on this earth. The chameleons are masters of camouflage who can change color to blend in with the color of their surroundings. Many lizards have detachable tails and have escaped death by leaving their tails in the grasp of a predator. Hognosed snakes first try to bluff predators by acting fierce, then turn over on their backs and play dead.

Poisonous snakes try to avoid unpleasant encounters with animals too large for them to overcome by advertising their toxicity. The coral snake's brightly colored body, the cobra's menacing hood, and the rattlesnake's rattle all serve notice to other animals that these snakes are to be avoided.

One of the most important survival features of vertebrates is a complex nerve control center—the brain. The reptile brain is more complex than the amphibian brain and coordinates a higher degree of movement. Crocodilians also show a higher degree of intelligence than amphibians and other reptiles. Intelligence is often con-

*Like all rattlesnakes, the diamondback
rattlesnake adds a horny segment to the end
of its tail each time it sheds its skin. The rattling
of these segments warns nearby animals to
stay away from this poisonous creature.*

sidered to mean that behavior is controlled less by instinct and more by the ability to evaluate information. Learned behavior is usually more valuable as a survival tool than instinct because it allows animals to adjust to an almost infinite variety of situations rather than the few that can be programmed by instinct.

Except for some areas of the desert, where they hold a survival advantage over mammals and where they encounter few humans, the dwindling ranks of the reptiles are threatened further by humans. Many species suffer greatly from the habitat destruction caused by the encroachment of civilization. Some species of sea turtles, land tortoises, and crocodiles have also been hunted to extinction; others are perilously close. Smaller, secretive, and less conspicuous reptiles remain in great numbers. But unless care is taken in how humans exploit their environment, tiny lizards and snakes will be all that is left of the animal group that has long been an important part of land-dwelling life.

# 4
# BIRDS

Little imagination is needed to see an evolutionary connection between a fish and an amphibian tadpole. The similarities between an amphibian salamander and a reptilian lizard are also obvious. But from that point, the history of the vertebrates takes a bizarre jump. How in the world do we get from crocodiles and turtles to goldfinches? How can crawling animals with scales be remotely related to flying animals with feathers?

Nonetheless, scientists believe that birds evolved from reptiles between 225 and 150 million years ago. A key support for this view came with the discovery of a missing link called an *archaeopteryx*. A fossil of an archaeopteryx dating back 140 million years showed a reptilelike animal with teeth, a tail bone, and birdlike feathers. Despite the lack of resemblance, feathers are made from the same substance as fish and lizard scales, a protein called *keratin*.

Some ancient reptiles such as the pteranodons

*This fossil of an archaeopteryx shows a
startling combination of a reptilian body
form and the characteristic feathers of a bird.*

gained survival advantages from the ability to fly. They could travel farther and faster and avoid difficult terrain. Birds arose as a successful group by finding more and better ways of exploiting this virtually untapped air environment. No one is certain how the first birds became airborne. But since most of the reptiles and mammals that travel through the air are tree-dwelling gliders, many experts speculate that birds evolved from similar tree-dwelling, gliding reptiles. At some stage, they suppose, those animals' ability to glide evolved into true flight.

Birds are perhaps the clearest examples of how animals acquire features according to the demands of their environment and life-style. The act of flight requires far different physical features than are important for running, climbing, jumping, or swimming. Eventually, the changes developed for more efficient flight led the ancestors of birds far away from the appearance and habits of reptiles. Today, the only obvious physical features that link birds and reptiles in a common ancestry are the scales on the legs of birds and the fact that both lay shelled eggs.

Feathers are the primary feature that sets birds apart from other animals. All birds have feathers; no other animal has them. One type of feather consists of a stiff shaft with many interlocking barbs that branch out from it to form a flat surface. These are of obvious advantage in flying. They are lightweight yet sturdy. They are streamlined to overcome air resistance yet have a large surface area for pushing against the air to generate lift and forward motion. Flight wings are firmly attached to the body to hold up against the powerful airflow encountered during flight.

It takes more than feathers, though, to transform a terrestrial animal into an efficient flyer. The forelimbs of birds have been modified into the shape of a wing which, like the feathers, is streamlined and has an increased surface area for pushing against air. Birds have also developed powerful flight muscles attached to the breastbone and the upper part of the wing. The downstroke muscles are the most crucial for most birds since they provide the lift. Flight muscles may account for 30 to 40 percent of the bird's total body weight. Smaller muscles are used for lifting and twisting the wings; this helps the bird change direction. Steering is also aided by the tail feathers, which act as a rudder.

Weight is one of the greatest obstacles to flight, and birds have trimmed off virtually all weight that is not absolutely necessary. Their bones are thin and hollow. A bald eagle's skeleton weighs only one-third as much as the total weight of its feathers. Some bird bones have become reduced in size, and some have fused with other bones. Teeth have been eliminated altogether.

The stress brought on by air turbulence during flight has made it advantageous for birds to have rigid bodies. As was evident with the turtles, however, rigid bodies lose the advantage of flexibility. To compensate for this, birds have developed a long, bendable neck. Not only does this flexible neck allow more mobility, but it also helps the bird to keep its head level. In this way, a bird can keep its bearings while its body twists in the air during flight.

With the exception of very light birds such as hummingbirds, a great deal of energy is required to overcome gravity and produce flight. In order to provide the high metabolism required to produce this energy, birds must make a great deal of oxygen available to their cells. The inefficient respiration systems of the amphibians would make flight virtually impossible for them. Even the reptiles, with their improved respiratory systems, would find flight difficult. Birds have boosted their respiration efficiency with the addition of air sacs. These air sacs, which are connected by tubes to the lungs, can be found in various places throughout the birds, including the hollow insides of bones. They help to create a one-way flow of air through the bird so that incoming air does not mix with outgoing air as occurs in other lung-breathing vertebrates. Birds breathe while at rest through the movements of rib and abdominal muscles that enlarge the body cavity so that it can draw in air. During flight, the action of the wings automatically raises and lowers the breastbone, causing air to be pumped in. Bird hearts tend to beat faster than those of other vertebrates—up to 500 times per minute in small birds, compared with fewer than 100 per minute in humans and 25 in some frogs.

The high *metabolism* required to produce energy for flight can occur only at high body temperatures. Since cold-blooded animals such as reptiles rely exclusively on the outside environment to provide body heat, this would further tend to limit flight in such creatures to tropical climates and low altitudes where the air is warmer.

An animal that could produce its own body heat, however, would not be so limited by the environment. Birds were able to free themselves from dependency on the sun for body warmth—they were probably the first warm-blooded animals. They maintain the highest internal temperature of all animals. All birds generate normal body temperatures of more than 100 degrees Fahrenheit (38°C), and many go above 110 degrees Fahrenheit (43°C) to facilitate their high metabolism. (Human body temperature averages between 98 and 99 degrees Fahrenheit.)

The enormous burden of providing the food and oxygen to stoke such high temperatures could be reduced if the animal were insulated; it could then hold on to much of the heat its body produces. The advantage of heat conservation has encouraged the modification of a type of feather quite different from the flight and contour feathers. These feathers, known as down, have soft, fluffy barbs that do not interlock. Down feathers are ideal for trapping body heat so that the bird stays warm. Baby chicks, whose food needs are provided for by the mother and for whom warmth is far more crucial than the ability to fly, have coats made entirely of down.

Down feathers could be of use only to an animal that generates heat from within. As insulators, they also prevent outside warmth from reaching the bird, which would be a severe disadvantage in a cold-blooded reptile that gains its body heat from the sun. Down insulation does more than maintain the warmth necessary for a bird to fly. It has enabled birds to invade climates too cold for reptiles and amphibians to tolerate.

In addition to branching far off from the reptiles in response to the requirements of flight, birds have developed many unique features among themselves in response to their environments. There are more than 8,000 recognized species of birds in existence today, ranging from the hummingbird, which weighs less than an ounce, to the 9-foot-tall (2.7 m), 300-pound (140 kg) ostrich. Birds have adjusted to every habitat imaginable, from the hottest desert to the frigid ice of Antarctica. They can be found soaring above the earth, diving under the water, or running across the grasslands.

Their diversity is so great that, unlike the reptiles, birds cannot be divided into a few easily recognizable orders, as a partial list of some of the more common orders shows:

Anseriformes—medium- to large-sized water birds with blunt, wide bills; these include ducks, geese, and swans.

Apodiformes—small, long-winged, fast-flying birds with very weak feet; these include swifts and hummingbirds.

Ciconiiformes—large, long-legged waders with long bills and necks; these include the herons.

Columbiformes—small-headed birds that spend much time on the ground and bob heads as they walk; these include pigeons and doves.

Falconiformes—hooked-beak, strong-clawed birds who hunt by day; these include eagles, hawks, and falcons.

Galliformes—thick-bodied, small-headed ground birds with short wings and strong legs for running; these include grouse, quail, and chickens.

Gruiformes—tall, long-legged marsh birds, thicker-bodied than herons; these include cranes.

Passeriformes—the most common order of birds, they have feet designed for perching and for standing on the ground; these include sparrows, crows, finches, wrens, and jays.

Piciformes—medium-sized birds with strong bills and skulls for drilling into wood; these include woodpeckers.

Strigiformes—broad-headed night-hunting birds with both eyes facing forward; these include owls.

Bird classification is a difficult science with few clear-cut divisions and many points of disagreement among experts. More than 5,000 species are lumped together in the Passeriformes, which some refer to as the perching birds and others as the songbirds.

Bird bodies are wonderful examples of adaptive radiation, so fine-tuned to their life-styles that it is possible to figure out a bird's living habits just from looking at three main features: the wings, beak, and feet.

Bird wings correspond to the birds' need for speed, power, or maneuverability. Swifts are small birds with long, narrow, streamlined wings and stiff tail feathers. These birds are built for speed. They flash through the air at high speeds while they devour insects in flight.

Condor wings can span nearly 10 feet (3 m) and are broad and heavy. A bird that tried to flap such wings continually and rapidly would expend a great deal of energy in flight. The vast surface area, though, makes condor wings well suited for soaring. These birds rise up in the sky on upcurrents of warm air, flapping occasionally, and then glide slowly as they look for dead animals to devour.

The grouse's wings are short and broad. Obviously, the grouse cannot be a soarer or a swift flyer. It lives on the ground, where it feeds on berries, plant buds, and an occasional crawling insect. The price that grouse pay for living among this rich assortment of food on the ground is that they are within easy reach of a variety of ground predators. Grouse wings provide power for explosive takeoffs that help the grouse escape the attacks of predators.

The owls' soft, closely packed wing feathers allow them to fly silently, a perfect feature for a bird that counts on the element of surprise to capture rodents. Hummingbird wings make the sound for which they are named. Their small wings beat too rapidly to be seen with the eye, and they are the only birds capable of flying backward. These wings are ideally suited for hovering around the flowers on which hummingbirds feed.

Those birds that are most exposed to water would most benefit from a coat of oil on their feathers to keep them from getting waterlogged. Not surprisingly, ducks and other waterfowl have glands that coat their feathers with oil. Penguins, which are unable to fly, are also especially streamlined so that they can "fly" through the water, where resistance is far greater than in the air.

A bird's beak is a good indicator of what type of food it eats. Swallows have wide mouths and small, weak beaks. Obviously, they do not eat anything that requires crushing or tearing. They primarily eat small flying insects that they can easily ingest whole. The reduced beak lightens their weight so they can fly faster, and their wide mouth gives them a better chance of capturing their prey at high speed.

Finches, cardinals, and grosbeaks have short, thick, strong beaks. Such a beak would be of little use in catching flying insects, but it is well suited for providing the crushing power to break open the seeds and nuts on which those birds live. Parrot beaks are even more vise-like. Some parrots can even crack open Brazil nuts.

Herons and kingfishers are equipped with long, daggerlike beaks. These are too narrow to be of much use in swallowing insects out of the sky and too weak to crack nuts on the ground. But they are perfect for piercing the water and seizing fish. Pelican beaks, with a pouch of skin at the base of the throat, are further specialized for fishing. A pelican can catch several fish on a single hunt by snatching a fish with its long beak, flipping it into the pouch, and going after another.

Ducks have flattened bills that are especially useful as strainers. Many ducks get their food by dredging up mud and sifting out small worms, crustaceans, and insects. At the same time, the duck bill is versatile enough to allow ducks to feed on alternate sources such as grains and berries. Flamingos are more specialized strainers. The oversized top half of their bill contains slits. Flamingos eat by stirring up mud with their feet and then bending over into the water to take in whatever is floating around. With their head in an upside-down position, they squeeze the water and mud out through their slits and filter out their food: algae and other water plants, as well as small animals.

The large, sharp, hooked beaks of eagles and hawks, and the smaller hooked beaks of owls, are designed for tearing flesh. They are needed by these hunting birds, who feed on rodents and other small mammals, reptiles, amphibians, fish, snails, and small birds, most of which must be torn into smaller pieces before they can be swal-

With legs and neck proportionately longer than any
other bird, the flamingo is well equipped to wade
into the water. There it strains water through its bill
in hopes of capturing small, floating morsels of food.

lowed. Beaks in hunting birds serve a purpose similar to teeth in reptiles.

Woodpecker bills look something like the daggerlike bills of the fish-eating herons and kingfishers, only stronger and sharper. These can be used as drills that penetrate bark and wood so the bird can reach the insects hidden inside. Hummingbird bills are longer, thinner, and more delicate. They are not designed for drilling wood but for penetrating deep into flower petals. Hummingbirds also have a long tongue that extends out through the bill to lap up the flower nectar on which they feed.

Many songbirds, such as robins, blackbirds, and orioles, have medium-sized beaks with no apparent specialization. These beaks are useful for a variety of easily ingested foods such as fruit, berries, worms, and ground insects.

Bird legs also show many adaptations that help them in their particular life-style. Most birds have four toes, three facing forward and one pointing toward the back. This helps them gain a grip on small landing spaces. Many perching birds have toes that can lock around a branch or twig. This allows them to sleep on their perches without danger of falling; in this way, they can remain out of the reach of ground predators. Some birds have small, weak feet suited only for perching, while others can support themselves on the ground as well as on branches.

Water birds, such as ducks, have flaps of skin between the toes. This provides a greater surface area for pushing against the water and helps to make them strong swimmers. Web-footed loons have been known to dive to depths of more than 180 feet (55 m). Shorebirds often have long, widely spread toes that help to keep them from sinking in soft sand and mud.

The ostrich is one of the few birds that cannot fly, and its legs and toes are adapted to generate running

*The black-chinned hummingbird, found in North and South America, obtains food with its long, slender bill. It spends much of its time eating since even at rest a hummingbird uses up twenty-five times as much energy as an animal such as a chicken.*

speed. Ostriches have only two toes, and their long legs cover a great deal of ground with each stride. Birds of prey such as owls and hawks are equipped with long, sharp claws for grasping and holding on to their struggling prey. Chickens have shorter, blunter claws that they use to scratch the ground in their search for food.

Bird senses have also developed in response to the requirements of flight. Their fast-moving, high-flying existence does not lend itself to a leisurely sampling of aromas. As a result, birds rely less on a sense of smell than do other vertebrates. Their uncluttered air environment, though, usually offers them a wide field of vision, and birds have exploited this to the fullest. Birds have the most advanced eyesight of any creature on earth. Hawks, eagles, and vultures can spot the movement of a small animal from several miles away.

Birds also communicate and obtain information about the presence of other members of their species through their ability to make sounds and to hear the sounds of others. Bird calls are so distinctive that many species can be identified solely from the sounds they make. These calls range from the beautiful, musical call of the warbler to the irritating caw of the crow.

The nervous systems of birds have to be highly developed to coordinate the complex movements and split-second alterations that occur in flight. Maintaining balance and correct body position are far more important to flying animals than to those anchored on the ground, and a large portion of the bird brain is concerned with controlling this function.

Birds, however, have a limited ability to learn behavior. Most of their behavior is based on instinct, which is a kind of programmed behavior built in at birth. Birds do not learn survival techniques such as how to build a nest or where to migrate. They are born with that basic knowledge.

Some instinctive behavior is incredibly elaborate. Many birds gather at a particular time of year to fly to breeding grounds hundreds and even thousands of miles away. The arctic tern instinctively migrates from near the Arctic Circle in the north to Antarctica in the south each year, a round trip of over 22,000 miles (35,000 km).

The digestive system of a bird has little to do with the process of flight, and so birds are similar in this regard to other vertebrates. Like the reptiles, birds do not chew their food; they rely exclusively on their internal digestive system to break down food. This occurs in two steps. Food is stored first in the crop, where it is broken down by enzymes. A second digestive section known as the *gizzard* grinds the food into smaller pieces. (Some birds even swallow stones to help the gizzard in this process.) As in all animals, because of the difficulty in breaking down plant material, birds that eat plant material such as grain have larger digestive systems than those that eat insects or animals.

Like the reptiles, birds reproduce by laying hard-shelled eggs, which can be fertilized only inside the female. This method of reproduction requires a male to pair with a female. Birds of opposite sex rely on vision and sound to get together for mating. In many species, males and females are quite different in appearance. Female hawks and owls are generally larger than the males. Male birds are among the most brightly colored animals on earth, and this brilliant display helps them to attract a female. Some male birds engage in complex courtship rituals to ensure the cooperation of the female. Prairie chickens are especially noted for their mating dance, which is accompanied by loud, booming calls. Many birds rely on their attraction techniques to obtain a new mate each mating season. Others have eliminated the need to constantly attract new mates by keeping the same partner for life.

Unlike the reptiles, most birds take an active part in caring for their young. Many of them build elaborate nests for their eggs. Because this is instinctive behavior,

*This Baltimore, or Northern, oriole feeds its young in an elaborate nest it has woven from grasses.*

birds of the same species will all build similar, but often distinctive, nests. Northern orioles weave a hanging basket from grasses. Swallows plaster mud into ledges and corners of cliffs and buildings. Eagles pile sticks into a huge nest high in trees or on cliffs. Loons build nests of mud and vegetation by the water. This construction is all the more remarkable because bird wings are too specialized for flight to be of any use in their building efforts. Birds must carry and work materials entirely with their beaks.

In order to keep the unhatched birds at the required high body temperature, parents incubate them with their own body heat. In most species, the female takes responsibility for lying on the eggs until they hatch. But flamingo eggs are incubated by both parents, and the most selfless incubators of all are the male emperor penguins. This bird stands for two months in the dark, frozen wastes of Antarctica, eating nothing and braving temperatures of minus 70 degrees Fahrenheit ($-57°C$) to keep the eggs warm.

Most species of birds develop so slowly that they are unable to survive on their own for a period after birth. The survival of these species can be ensured only by continued parental care. Many birds spend a great deal of time and energy finding food for their young. Some parents, especially among birds that nest on the ground, will risk their own lives to draw predators away from the nest, often pretending to be injured and thus seemingly easy prey.

The care provided by parents guarantees that a large percentage of bird eggs will hatch and grow into adults. As a result, birds do not lay as many eggs as do fish, amphibians, and most reptiles. An ostrich may lay up to twenty eggs, but most perching birds lay fewer than half a dozen. Eagles commonly lay only a couple of eggs, and some flamingos lay only one at a time.

By and large, birds have been a successful group

of vertebrates that have adapted to every climate and environment on earth. As with most vertebrates, the greatest threat to their existence comes from humans. Passenger pigeons were once perhaps the most numerous birds in the world. Their migrations filled the sky for hours from one horizon to another. In the early twentieth century, however, these creatures were hunted to extinction. Today, many water birds suffer from the destruction of their habitats as developers drain marshes to make the land more suitable for human needs. Other species of birds are endangered by human pollution in the form of toxic chemicals, oil spills, and acid rain.

# 5
# MAMMALS

While fish reign in the waters of the earth, and birds are the undisputed masters of the air, mammals have dominated the land masses of the world since taking over from the dinosaurs.

Perhaps 200 million years ago a branch of reptiles, building on the improvements and modifications honed by countless generations of animals over the years, began to develop the marvelously efficient and flexible mammalian body plan. While insignificant compared to the awesome dinosaurs, these mammals were able to adjust to the changing conditions that might have eliminated the dinosaurs some 65 million years ago.

The basic mammal body form is so well engineered that it has been adapted to virtually all environments. Mammals can be found digging underground, flying through the air, hanging from trees, or racing across open plains. They live in the bitter cold of the Arctic, the blazing heat of the desert, and the sunless depths miles

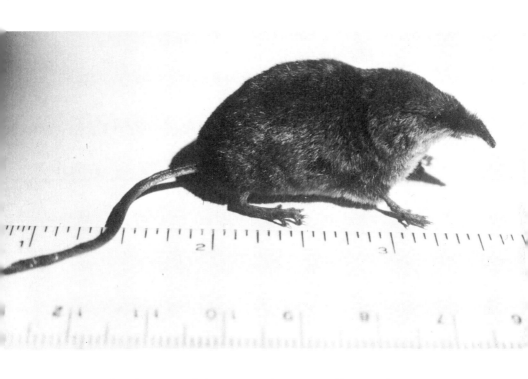

*The diversity of the mammal group is illustrated by the difference in sizes of this tiny wandering shrew, which can weigh less than one-tenth of an ounce (2 g), and the enormous blue whale, which can tip the scales at 120 tons (109,000 kg).*

below the ocean surface. So diverse is the mammal group that it contains both the porcupine, that unwieldy four-legged pincushion of the forest, and the dolphin, the graceful, legless acrobat of the sea. It includes both the ferocious tiger and the timid rabbit. The pigmy shrew, a tiny insect eater weighing only a fraction of an ounce, and the 120-ton blue whale, the largest animal ever to inhabit the earth, share the characteristics of the mammal. The basic mammal plan has provided one of its

83

species, *Homo sapiens*, with the ability to so alter and control its environment that it has disrupted the natural checks and balances that have governed populations since the first animals appeared.

The most obvious physical features that separate mammals from the rest of the animal kingdom are hair and *mammary glands*. At first glance, neither may seem to be significant factors in survival, but they do provide advantages.

Hair on mammals acts as an insulator. In this regard it serves the same purpose as feathers on birds and, in fact, is formed out of the same keratin substance that produces feathers. Like birds, mammals are warm-blooded creatures who generate body heat from within. Warm-bloodedness frees mammals from total dependence on the sun to maintain their body temperatures.

Producing internal heat, however, requires a great deal of energy. Hair reduces the amount of energy a mammal must use in producing heat by preventing much internal warmth from escaping. With a few exceptions, for example, the whales, in which hair has been reduced to a few bristles, all mammals have hair. Those that live in the coldest climates, such as musk oxen and arctic hares, generally have the thickest, best-insulating fur. Many mammals who live in lands with changing seasons can shed fur in the summer and grow a thick coat for extra warmth in the winter. Animals such as the arctic hare gain an extra survival advantage from this shedding by wearing a white winter coat that blends in with snow and a brown one that helps them hide from predators in the summer.

In tropical jungles and deserts, where heat is readily available to cold-blooded animals, fur-insulated warm-bloodedness offers mammals no advantage over their terrestrial rivals, the reptiles and amphibians. As a result, mammals are less dominant in these locations.

But mammals have enjoyed great success in colder

The musk ox, hunted to near extinction in
the nineteenth century, is an example of a
mammal that has adapted to its cold climate
by developing thick, well-insulated fur.

climates. The ability of mammals to tolerate colder conditions may explain why mammals survived the environmental changes that might have led to the extinction of the dinosaurs. Some mammals further combat harsh weather by reverting to the tactic of hibernating found in the older animal groups. During their months of hibernation, the sleeping animals' metabolism slows down almost to a standstill. Virtually no energy is required to maintain a system in such a state, and so their body temperature may dip to a few degrees above freezing without harming them.

The mammary glands from which the mammals get their name are a specialized method of providing nutrition for the young. These glands produce milk, a substance rich in protein, vitamins, and calcium. The exact content of the milk varies from species to species, but in each case provides the combination of nutrients best suited to promote growth in that species. Milk production, which occurs only in the females, is stimulated by the sucking action of the young. This system ensures that the mother's energy goes into milk production only when a child is in need of it.

Besides providing an exceptionally high-quality food source, the mammary glands offer protection to the young. At the time in their lives when they are most helpless, young mammals do not have to expose themselves to predators by going out in search of food. Nor do their parents have to leave them unprotected while they find food for their young as many birds must do. Suckling mammals can satisfy their food needs while under the protective shadow of a parent.

A more subtle but important advantage enjoyed by mammals over reptiles is in their teeth. The fearsome, razor-sharp teeth of a tyrannosaur may seem like the ultimate eating equipment; they actually have only a limited use. Reptiles have only one kind of tooth, one

*This nursing white-tailed fawn is both
fed and protected by its mother.*

whose purpose is to seize prey or to shear off chunks
small enough to swallow. They do not chew food. This
means that a reptile's food enters its digestive system
unaltered. When a stomach has to break down raw,
unprocessed food into a usable form, the process is slow
and time consuming. Several weeks may be required for

a snake to digest a single meal. During this time, when the body's energy is concentrated on digestion, reptiles are often sluggish and less able to defend themselves.

Mammals have various kinds of teeth, many of which are designed to break down the food into a form that can be quickly and easily digested. *Incisors* are located at the front of the mouth and are used for biting. *Canines*, similar to shearing reptile teeth, can be found on the sides. Flat-topped *molars*, the grinding teeth that chew the food into smaller pieces, are located toward the rear.

Mammal teeth are adapted to the type of food an animal eats. Tigers, wolves, and other predators of large animals have long, sharp canines that help grip the prey and tear it to pieces. Plant eaters have no use for such teeth and may lack them altogether. Cows, elephants, and other eaters of soft plants rely on large molars to crush and soften the plants. Browsers such as deer use their lower incisors to help clip off plants. Animals such as beavers and mice that gnaw through harder material are equipped with exceptionally large incisors for that purpose. Mammals, such as humans, that eat a wide variety of foods have an ample supply of each kind of tooth.

Mouth shape in mammals may also reflect their eating habits. The white rhinoceros is a grazer and has a blunt snout well suited for eating grass. The black rhino, which prefers to browse on shrubs, has a more pointed snout and a more flexible upper lip that can pull branches into the mouth.

Many mammals also have digestive tracts that allow them to make use of hard-to-digest plant foods unavailable to reptiles. Cows, for example, must eat enormous quantities of grasses in order to gain the necessary nutrients from this low-quality food source. Digestion of all this tough material would be virtually impossible for a simple, one-chambered digestive system. Cows process food with a four-chambered digestive tract. Plant mate-

*The aggressive snarl of this wolf makes it possible
to see its well-developed canine teeth clearly.*

rial is swallowed into storage chambers where the cellulose is broken down by microorganisms. From time to time, the food can be regurgitated to the mouth for further chewing, and then moved further along the digestive tract.

The many digestive storage chambers also allow animals to eat a great deal of food quickly. This reduces the time that grazing animals stand with their heads down, exposed to predators. They can complete their chewing at a later time from a safer position.

Food-gathering and digesting adaptations are especially important to mammals because they must consume far greater amounts of food than reptiles in order to fuel their internal furnace. Shrews, for example, must eat their own weight in food each day just to survive.

Mammals have retained the basic four-legged, five-digit construction of the reptiles for mobility, but they have adapted it for their needs. Mammals are the swiftest runners in nature, using leg bones and muscles that work together as levers to provide motion. In most, the hind legs are more powerful and provide most of the push, while front legs provide a landing surface and a secondary push.

The easiest way to increase speed in a running animal is to lengthen the legs. Many of the swiftest animals, such as antelope and cheetahs, have developed long, slender legs. Horses have extended the length of their legs by raising up on their toes, developing hooves in the process. Horses have also enhanced their speed by reducing the number of digits, thus decreasing the amount of resistance each time a hoof touches the ground. The swiftest animals are found on the open plains, where there is nowhere to hide and speed is necessary to overcome prey and to escape from predators.

The hind-leg push is exaggerated in such animals as kangaroos and rabbits, whose enlarged hind legs provide almost all the motion, a form of movement called hopping.

The four-legged structure has proved adaptable to a wide variety of environments and types of movement. Tree-dwelling animals such as squirrels are skilled climbers. Bats, by adding a membrane of skin that stretches between the elongated fingers of their forearms and shorter hind legs, are capable of sustained flight. Seals have developed legs in the form of flippers that help the animals to swim easily through the water, yet allow them to move on land. Whales, which have no need of land locomotion, have become even more streamlined in response to the demands of the water, losing their rear appendages altogether.

The five-digit limbs retained by mammals as diverse as raccoons, monkeys, and humans have also proven especially useful for survival. They simplify the task of grasping objects, are useful for climbing, and give humans the dexterity to shape the environment to their advantage. Most mammals also have a tail that may serve a variety of functions, ranging from balance to climbing to swatting pests.

Besides being the fastest runners and most dexterous manipulators of the environment, mammals are also the largest animals in the world. The blue whale, which spans over 100 feet (30 m) and may weigh over 120 tons, is the largest animal to ever inhabit the earth. Size is a great survival advantage to an individual simply because, all other things being equal, small animals find it difficult to kill larger ones. The elephant, which may weigh more than 7 tons and is by far the largest land animal in the world, has no natural enemies.

Great size, however, places heavy demands on a number of body structures and functions. The larger the animal, the stronger the support system must be to prevent the animal from collapsing under its own weight. Whales have the advantage of being surrounded by water that is dense enough to help support their tremendous weight. Beached whales often quickly die simply because their unsupported weight crushes their own organs.

Land mammals have nothing but their own body structure to support their weight. Elephants must rely on massive, stumplike legs to provide them with a stable base. This cuts down on their mobility because such legs can't be used to jump or turn quickly. Even the massive frame of an elephant would not be able to support the weight of its huge head if it weren't for the fact that its skull is filled with air cells and channels that reduce its weight.

An even greater obstacle to size among animals is the demand for oxygen. Most tiny creatures are able to bring needed oxygen to their cells simply by absorbing oxygen from the outside through the cell membranes. Many of the cells of larger animals, though, are surrounded by other cells and have no direct access to outside oxygen. Fish have developed gills, and reptiles and birds lungs, to bring oxygen into the body, where it can be distributed to cells by the blood. The larger the animal, the more difficult it is for those respiratory systems to reach all the cells. Since all mammals have lungs and breathe air, oxygen supply is a particular challenge for large mammals that live in the sea.

Mammals have responded by developing a useful way of bringing in air, more efficient lungs, and a more efficient heart. The heart and lungs are separated from other internal organs by a *diaphragm*, a thin sheet of muscle connected to the ribs and other muscles. When this diaphragm is pulled down, it greatly enlarges the chest cavity, like a bellows, and easily draws in a large quantity of air.

The lungs are a complex system of tubes that repeatedly branch into smaller tubes. Air enters the body through a large tube called the *trachea*, which splits into the two bronchial tubes, each of which leads to one of the paired lungs. These tubes branch into smaller and smaller tubes until they end up in tiny sacs called *alveoli*. Alveoli are so thin that oxygen from the air can diffuse through them into the bloodstream, where it is carried to other cells. The millions of alveoli spread throughout the lungs provide an enormous surface area for this exchange of gas. The rate of breathing is controlled by the level of waste carbon dioxide in the blood.

The mammal's four-chambered heart then makes

certain that this distribution of oxygen is carried out efficiently. One chamber of the heart collects the oxygen-depleted blood; a second chamber pumps it to the lungs to gather oxygen. After this occurs, the blood returns to the other side of the heart and is pumped out to the body.

Seals and whales have developed even more efficient ways of supplying their cells with oxygen. Seals can empty their lungs far more completely than most other animals when they exhale, and so take in more oxygen when they inhale. Whales store oxygen in the blood-stream for use on deep dives that can last as long as an hour.

Mammals have continued the vertebrate tendency to develop keen senses to gain information from their surroundings. Although their eyesight is not as sharp as the birds', many mammals, particularly the hunters, can see well. Sense of smell is more important to other mammals. Dogs are well known for their ability to track down individuals by the faint scent they leave behind. Rabbits often sample the air with their noses to detect the presence of predators.

Other animals rely more heavily on their sense of hearing. Elephants and deer are quick to pick up faint sounds that might signal danger. Whales communicate with an elaborate system of underwater calls. Bats have so refined the art of hearing that they use it to find their way in the dark. They send out high-pitched sounds and can detect the presence of rocks, walls, and insects from the echo of these sounds off those objects.

Mammal use of the sense of touch may be best demonstrated by the walrus, whose sensitive facial hairs detect the presence of mollusks it stirs up from the ocean bottoms with its tusks, by human fingers, and by elephant trunks that are sensitive to differences in temperature and texture.

Mammals reproduce sexually with internal fertilization. Males and females are attracted to each other for this purpose by smell, sound, and sight. Many female mammals have only brief periods during the year when they are able to conceive. This can provide certain advantages. It ensures that the young are born during mild weather when food is more available, and it conserves energy that would be wasted in a continual readiness for fertilization. Chemical attractants from the females alert males as to when the females are "in heat," or ready for mating.

Like the birds, mammals also facilitate mating by means of *secondary sexual characteristics*, physical features that accent the differences between the sexes. In most mammals, size is the primary difference, with the males generally larger. Among the deer family, however, males display large ornamental antlers. Male lions are easily distinguished from females by the hairy mane that fringes their faces.

Male mammals often compete over the right to mate with females. In these fights, the larger and stronger males prevail. This offers the species the survival advantage of passing on the genetic traits of the stronger animals.

A key feature that distinguishes most mammals from other vertebrates is that their young develop inside a womb and are born live. While inside the mother, they are nourished by a *placenta*, an organ richly supplied with blood that provides nutrients from the mother's body.

The importance of this can be seen by looking at the success of three different groups of mammals who share all the other mammalian features except the manner of birth. *Monotremes* include the bizarre-looking platypus, a hairy, duck-billed animal with webbed feet. This animal digs underground nests, but spends much of its time in the water looking for food, which it locates with the sensitive skin of its bill. Like other mammals, the platypus gives milk to its young. Unlike other mammals, though,

*The large ornamental antlers of the male mule deer distinguish it from the female deer.*

it lays eggs. Despite having all other mammalian advantages, monotremes are among the rarest animals on earth; they are found in only a small range in the South Pacific.

*Marsupials* have replaced egg laying with live birth, but do not have a placenta. Instead, they give birth to tiny, poorly developed young, who attach themselves to a pouch on the mother's abdomen and are nourished by her milk. Opossums no larger than a bee are born within two weeks of fertilization. Even the great gray kangaroo gives birth to inch-long young.

The most developed features of newborn marsupials are their forelimbs and nerves, which allow them to locate the mother's pouch and crawl to it. There they feed on their mother's milk for two months or more until fully developed. Some kangaroos produce only one baby at a time, while a mother opossum can raise as many as thirteen young, one for each of her teats.

Marsupials are equipped with many of the survival advantages of other mammals. Opossums have an excellent sense of smell. Kangaroos can bound across the plain as fast as most running mammals. Yet marsupials are scarce. Most are limited to the far reaches of the earth, with the Virginia opossum being the only marsupial in North America.

Both monotremes and marsupials have been crowded out of most locations by the other type of mammal, the *eutherians*—those whose young develop inside the mother, nourished by the placenta. The relative success of eutherians compared to monotremes and marsupials lends strong support to the idea that placental birth offers survival advantages. The womb provides a safe place for the vulnerable young to develop; it is a far safer place than an egg. Unlike the birds, mammals are not confined to laying on the eggs to keep them warm. Placental mammals can go about obtaining what they need for survival while the embryo stays warm inside the body. The womb provides such protection to the offspring that many mammals need produce only one baby at a time, as compared to the multiple births of other vertebrates.

Eutherian fetuses can also enjoy a far longer period of development. They receive a greater supply of nourishment from the mother than the limited amount of food that can be stored inside an egg. The long development period makes it possible for large mammals to attain a reasonable proportion of their adult size at birth. While small mammals such as mice may require only three weeks in the womb, elephants, whales, and rhinos develop in the mother for nearly two years.

Due to a long *gestation* period, some animals are well developed at birth. A newborn giraffe, for example, can stand on its long legs twenty minutes after birth. Newborn horses can follow their mothers within hours of birth. Pronghorns can outrun humans before they are four days old.

In other mammals, the longer development period before birth allows the young to develop more complex physical features. This is one factor leading to the rise of another mammalian advantage, the development of a complex nervous system. Mammals have developed a large brain that can sort out the millions of messages provided by the senses and store them for further use. While other vertebrates rely heavily on ingrained instinct to govern their behavior, most mammals have at least some ability to learn, to alter their behavior based on the information they receive from the environment.

This ability can be a great survival advantage. Foxes, wolves, and bears are notorious for their ability to recognize signs of a trap, and so can easily avoid them. Young predators can learn hunting skills both from their parents and from their own successes and failures. The most dramatic result of this ability to learn, of course, has been the dominance of humans. The development of language and the powers of reason have enabled humans to overcome animals of far greater strength, and to control and shape their environment far beyond what any other creature has ever achieved.

The success of the mammalian body plan can be seen in the number and variety of orders that make up the class. A sample of some of the more common orders includes:

Artiodactyla—distinguished from the Perisso-dactyla (see below) by their feet, which have an even number of digits. This order includes deer, cattle, sheep, antelope, and pigs.

Carnivora—a wide-ranging group of primarily meat-eating animals that includes the members of the cat and dog families, as well as weasels and bears. All have both eyes located in the front of the skull for binocular vision and have a keen sense of smell. They include some of the most powerful land animals on earth—bears and tigers. Cats tend to hunt alone by stealth and quickness, while most canines, including dogs and wolves, prefer hunting in packs. Otters are especially adapted to hunting in water.

Cetacea—mammals so adapted to the sea that they have become completely aquatic, to the point where they have lost their hind limbs and almost all of their hair. The whales and dolphins of this group are known for their intelligence. Blue whales feed by straining out tons of small crustaceans from the water. Sperm whales can dive miles beneath the ocean surface to capture giant squid.

Chiroptera—bats, the only mammal group capable of sustained flight. They may have developed this ability as well as their echolocation hearing (the ability to locate objects by emitting high-pitched sounds and listening for the echo reflected from objects the sounds strike) in response to the availability of night-flying insects. Birds, which rely primarily on keen eyesight, could not take advantage of this food source and so left the field wide open for an insect eater that not only could fly but also hunt at night.

Edentata—animals that have lost their teeth and instead have developed mouths and tongues more suited to capturing soft, small-bodied prey, primarily insects. This group includes anteaters and armadillos.

Insectivora—small mammals that feed on insects. Moles are especially adapted for living underground. Although sightless, they have sensitive feelers and strong front claws for digging. The group also includes the shrews and hedgehogs.

Perissodactyla—a group of large herbivores whose feet have an odd number of toes. The group includes the horse and rhinoceros.

Pinnipeda—mammals adapted for life on both land and sea. This group, which includes seals, sea lions, and walruses, has forelimbs streamlined into flippers.

Primates—an order characterized by adaptations for living in trees—such as hands that are used for grasping—and a tendency toward increased brain size and intelligence. The order includes tree shrews, monkeys, apes, and humans.

Rodentia—the most numerous mammals, thanks to their rapid rate of reproduction. Although many include insects and even small animals in their diets, rodents are distinguished by their sharp incisors, with which they bite and gnaw plants. Beavers are large rodents that have developed a complex behavior of dam building that allows them to reshape their environment to their needs. The rodent also includes mice, rats, squirrels, and porcupines.

The success of mammals in recent times has been tempered by the influence of humans, who have been especially destructive to fellow mammals. The bison, which once thundered across the western plains of North America in the millions, were so carelessly slaughtered that fewer than a thousand remained at the turn of the century. More than a quarter of a million blue whales roamed the oceans a century ago. Now there are so few left that many experts believe nothing can be done to prevent their extinction. Due to a combination of over-hunting, habitat destruction, and pollution, nearly one out of every ten mammal species is considered endangered. Most of the large mammals that remain are confined to remote wilderness areas or protected game parks.

# GLOSSARY

**Acanthopterygii.** Bony fish whose fins are supported by a series of thin, bony rays.

**Adaptive radiation.** The tendency of species within a group of animals to develop different physical features in response to different living conditions.

**Agnatha.** Fish without jaws.

**Alveoli.** Tiny air cells in the lungs through which oxygen is absorbed into the bloodstream and through which carbon dioxide is passed out of the bloodstream.

**Ammocoete.** The wormlike, larval form of the lamprey.

**Anura.** A group of tailless amphibians including frogs and toads.

**Apoda.** Aquatic or burrowing amphibians in which the legs have been reduced or lost altogether.

**Archaeopteryx.** An extinct animal whose fossils show a mixture of reptile characteristics such as teeth, and bird characteristics such as feathers.

**Barbels.** Wispy, whiskerlike sensors located on the faces of fish.

**Bioluminescence.** The ability of animals to produce light from reactions within the body.

**Caecilians.** Another name for members of the Apoda group.

**Camouflage.** The external appearance of an animal that allows it to blend in with its surroundings and avoid detection.

**Canines.** The long, sharp teeth also known as fangs; used by carnivores for tearing flesh.

**Cartilage.** The hard but elastic supportive skeletal structure found in many vertebrates. It is most commonly found in very young or formative stages of vertebrates but makes up virtually the entire internal skeleton of sharks.

**Chondrichthyes.** The group of fishes with jaws whose body skeletons are composed of cartilage.

**Chordata.** A phylum that includes all animals with a notochord, an elastic rod that extends down the length of their back; includes the vertebrates.

**Cold-blooded.** Relying on the environment to provide body warmth.

**Crocodilia.** An order of large, strong-swimming reptiles with powerful jaws and tails; includes crocodiles and alligators.

**Diaphragm.** A thin sheet of muscle and connective tissue that separates the chest from the abdomen in mammals.

**Eutherians.** Mammals in which the young develop in the mother's womb, nourished by a placenta.

**Gestation.** The period of growth from conception until birth by the young inside a mother's body.

**Gizzard.** The digestive cavity in birds; used for grinding food.

**Hibernation.** A condition in which the body's activity is drastically slowed down. This extreme inactivity by an animal during harsh seasons, particularly winter, eliminates its need to go out into an unfavorable environment to find food.

**Incisors.** The sharp, rectangular front teeth designed for biting, clipping, or gnawing.

**Keratin.** A protein from which external physical features such as scales, feathers, and hair are produced.

**Lateral line.** A line of specialized sensory cells running the length of a fish's body about midway up its sides; capable of detecting water turbulence caused by other animals.

**Mammary gland.** A characteristic gland of mammals that produces milk for the nourishment of their young.

**Marsupials.** Mammals that give live birth to undeveloped young; the young then spend a further period of development in the mother's pouch.

**Metabolism.** The chemical activity within living cells that provides growth and energy.

**Metamorphosis.** An often dramatic physical change from a larval form into an adult form.

**Molars.** The broad, flat-topped teeth designed for crushing and grinding.

**Monotremes.** Mammals who reproduce by laying eggs.

**Notochord.** A solid, elastic rod that provides support along the length of a chordate's body.

**Operculum.** The scaled flap that covers the gills in the bony fishes.

**Osteichthyes.** Fishes with jaws whose body skeleton is primarily composed of bone.

**Phylum.** One of the major divisions into which scientists divide the animal kingdom.

**Placenta.** An organ in eutherian mammals through which the mother passes on nourishment to the fetus in her womb.

**Rhynchocephalia.** An ancient order of lizardlike reptiles, only one of which (the tuatara) survives to this day.

**Secondary sexual characteristics.** Physical features that serve to attract members of the opposite sex for the purpose of mating.

**Sexual dimorphism.** The trait of developing physical features that distinguishes males from females.

**Shoal.** A large group of fish.

**Species.** The smallest group into which living things are classified. Members of a species have many characteristics in common and are able to interbreed.

**Squamata.** The order of long, thin reptiles that includes lizards and snakes.

**Streamlined.** Having a smooth, flowing shape that allows air or water to flow past with a minimum of resistance.

**Toxicity.** The level of poisonousness.

**Trachea.** The main tube in the air passage leading to the lungs.

**Tunicate.** A small, aquatic chordate related to the vertebrates.

**Urodela.** Four-legged amphibians with tails; these include salamanders and newts.

**Warm-blooded.** Producing body heat internally rather than relying on the outside environment to provide warmth.

# BIBLIOGRAPHY

Alderton, David. *Turtles and Tortoises of the World*. New York: Facts on File, 1988.

Alexander, R. McNeill. *Encyclopedia of Animal Biology*. New York: Facts on File, 1987.

*The Animal World*. Chicago: World Book, 1985.

*The Audubon Society's Encyclopedia of Animal Life*. New York: Clarkson Potter, 1982.

Bannister, Keith, and Andrew Campbell, eds. *Encyclopedia of Aquatic Life*. New York: Facts on File, 1985.

Berry, R. J., and A. Hallam. *The Encyclopedia of Animal Evolution*. New York: Facts on File, 1987.

Burnie, David. *Birds*. New York: Knopf, 1988.

Feduccia, Alan. *The Age of Birds*. Cambridge, Mass.: Harvard University Press, 1980.

Halliday, Tim R., and Kraig Adler, eds. *The Encyclopedia of Reptiles and Amphibians*. New York: Facts on File, 1986.

Macdonald, David, ed. *Encyclopedia of Mammals*. New York: Facts on File, 1984.

McCarthy, Colin. *Reptiles*. New York: Knopf, 1991.

Moyle, Peter B., and Joseph J. Cech, Jr. *Fishes: An Introduction to Ichthyology*. Englewood Cliffs, N.J.: Prentice-Hall, 1982.

Nelson, Joseph S. *Fishes of the World*. New York: Wiley, 1984.

Nowak, Ronald M. *Walker's Mammals of the World*, 5th ed. Baltimore: Johns Hopkins University Press, 1991.

Parker, Steve. *Fish*. New York: Knopf, 1990.

Patent, Dorothy Hinshaw. *The Challenge of Extinction*. Hillside, N.J.: Enslow, 1991.

Perrins, Christopher M., and Alex L. A. Middleton. *Birds*. New York: Facts on File, 1985.

# INDEX

—  —  —